Folk
Saints
of the Borderlands

Folk
Saints
of the Borderlands

Victims, Bandits & Healers

JAMES S. GRIFFITH

Rio Nuevo Publishers
Tucson, Arizona

To the people of the borderlands,
whose survival strategies are the subject of this book,
in deep gratitude for all that you have shared with me.

RIO NUEVO PUBLISHERS
P.O. Box 5250
Tucson, Arizona 85703-0250
(520) 623-9558
www.rionuevo.com

Design: Dawn Sokol
Map and decorative "milagros": Meghan Merker

Front cover: Teresa Urrea (from the Holden Collection/Special Collections Library at Texas Tech University, used here and on page 43 with permission), plus images of Juan Soldado, Pancho Villa, and Don Pedrito (all taken from prayer cards) • Back cover: Malverde Chapel in Culiacán (top right) and a monument to El Niño Fidencio on the road to Espinazo (bottom left) • Note: All field photography in this book is © James S. Griffith.

Library of Congress Cataloging-in-Publication Data

Griffith, James S.
  Folk saints of the borderlands : victims, bandits & healers / James S. Griffith.—1st American pbk. ed.
      p. cm.
Includes bibliographical references and index.
  ISBN 1-887896-51-1 (pbk.)
  1. Mexican-American Border Region—Religious life and customs. 2. Saints—Cult—Mexican-American Border Region. I. Title.
  BL2530.M39G75 2003
  235'.2'09721—dc21   2003011982

Printed in the United States of America

10 9 8 7 6 5 4 3 2 1

Author's note: Many of the Spanish phrases quoted in the book came from grave inscriptions and printed materials containing errors in grammar and inconsistent use of accent marks. I have intentionally presented those texts exactly as I found them, discrepancies and all.

CONTENTS

CHAPTER 1

THE SETTING

& the Cast of Thousands

In December 1982, Richard Morales and I were driving along the main highway about sixty miles south of the U.S./Mexico border, near Magdalena, Sonora. We noticed a small white chapel beside the road. A sign over the door read EL ANIMA DE JUAN SOLDADO ("the spirit of Juan Soldado").

"Who's Juan Soldado?" I asked Richard. He had never heard of him, so we stopped the car and walked to the ranch house behind the chapel to try to find out. That stop led us not only to the story of Juan Soldado but to information concerning other deceased men and women considered for one reason or another to be powerful helpers by many working-class Mexicans and Mexican Americans along the border. This book tells of the six most popular of those folk saints—or *ánimas* (spirits), as many people call them—as well as mentioning a few lesser-known ones.

Before we go any further, however, I need to fill in some background. The stories—and we will explore some wonderful ones—will come later, but if they are to be more than just stories, if they are to tell us more than their own narrative details, we need to place them in some sort of cultural and historical context.

MEXICAN CATHOLICISM

When the Spaniards arrived in Mexico in 1519, memories of the religious wars against the Moors were still fresh in their national consciousness. The militant Catholicism of that effort easily carried over to two other campaigns: the Counter-Reformation, and the conquest and conversion of the "heathen" lands of the Americas and elsewhere. For most Spaniards of the sixteenth century and later, the agendas of church and state were inseparable. Cortés carried an image of the Virgin with him and took every opportunity to explain the beliefs and narratives of Christianity to the native leaders he met. As soon as the military conquest ended in the Valley of Mexico, missionaries arrived and began their work of conversion. This "spiritual conquest," carried out by mendicants and supported by the Spanish Crown, continued long after the physical conquest was finished. While the Spanish expected that in a relatively few years, the natives would be transformed into Christian, tax-paying subjects of the Crown, the results were in truth somewhat different. Today, almost five centuries after the Spaniards arrived, many indigenous groups hold on to some vestiges of their traditional cultures and worldviews.

The Juan Soldado Capilla on Highway 15, south of Magdalena, Sonora, Mexico, in its last, most elaborate manifestation. (May 2000)

Mexico is scattered with native Christianities—the result of different indigenous groups selectively adopting aspects of Christianity, particularly behaviors that were enforceable by the missionaries, or beliefs and stories that resonated with their own cultures. Many of the native peoples of Mexico follow such religious systems, and anthropologists have studied and reported on many of them in a rich and fascinating literature. The Tohono O'odham (formerly known as the Papago Indians), who reside mostly in Arizona, with a few remaining in the Sonoran portion of their homeland, follow such a spiritual path. So do the Yaquis, whose homeland is in southern Sonora but who maintain communities elsewhere in that state as well as in southern Arizona. Such groups, however, make up a relatively small percentage of Mexico's population, which is predominantly mestizo in both race and culture. Traces of pre-Hispanic beliefs and practices are still present over much of Mexico, to be sure, even among apparently non-indigenous populations. But they remain traces, incorporated into what is basically a Catholic worldview.

When one describes Mexico as a Catholic country, much remains to be said. To be sure, Mexico has remained predominantly Catholic since the time of the Spanish Conquest, despite serious inroads in the twentieth century by other religious groups. But Mexican Catholicism itself comes in a wide variety of shapes and colors. For example, many Mexicans use five, rather than four, gestures to make the sign of the cross. The thumb and forefinger of the right hand are formed into the shape of a cross, and that cross is kissed after it is touched to the forehead, the breast, and the left and right shoulders. On a deeper level of meaning is the strong Mexican devotion to the Virgin of Guadalupe, and, indeed, to all aspects of Mary. This is not a recent phenomenon, as attested to by the mission church of San Xavier del Bac, just south of Tucson, Arizona, which still has most of the religious images from the time of its dedication in 1797. The church holds seventeen different images of Our Lady, and the Virgin's monogram appears six times on the walls of the church. She thus appears, at least

The Virgin of Guadalupe (La Virgen de Guadalupe or Nuestra Señora de Guadalupe) is the Virgin Mary as she is believed to have appeared to the Indian Juan Diego (now *Saint* Juan Diego, as of August 2002). The year was 1531, the place, the hill of Tepeyac—a site just outside Mexico City formerly considered sacred to the Aztec goddess Tonantzin, "Our Mother." She desired Juan Diego to tell the bishop that she wished a church in her honor be built on the site. When the bishop demanded proof, she told Juan Diego to gather up the roses that he found blooming on the hill (in December!) in his *tilma* or cloak and take them to the bishop. When Juan Diego dumped the roses at the bishop's feet, all were astonished to discover an image of the Virgin mysteriously imprinted on the tilma. This tilma now hangs behind the altar of the Basílica de Guadalupe in a suburb of Mexico City. The Virgin of Guadalupe is the most

Here she appears painted on a cliff face along Highway 15, just south of Magdalena, Sonora. (October 1999)

beloved supernatural figure in all of Mexico to this day, and her image appears virtually everywhere. She is traditionally identified as the protectress of the lowly and disenfranchised. Her banner was carried by the Insurgents in the War of Independence, by the revolutionary troops of Emiliano Zapata in the Mexican Revolution, and by members of César Chávez' United Farm Workers movement in the United States in the 1960s and 70s.

symbolically, twenty-three times. Mexico shares this Marian emphasis, of course, with much of Latin America, but it is certainly a characteristic of Mexican Catholicism that the Virgin Mother of God is omnipresent and extremely popular in all her manifestations, even among upper-class, educated Catholics.

The Catholicism of the upper and professional classes in Mexico probably comes closest to the international norms of the Catholic Church. As we move downwards on the Mexican socioeconomic scale, we also move farther and farther from the formal teachings of the contemporary Church, and enter a system that, though fully Catholic in its basic values and narratives, seems to have as a primary purpose survival in a hostile world. Another world, however, occupied by potential helpers and potential enemies, is also close at hand. Supernatural help is freely called upon, and dangers such as witchcraft are real and can be dealt with. Much of this emphasis would not seem strange to mainstream Catholics of the seventeenth and eighteenth centuries; the missionaries and those who followed them did their work well in Mexico. However, few of the changes in official Church thought that took place during the twentieth century, and especially since the Second Vatican Council of 1967, have truly permeated the world of the Mexican poor. The Mass has changed, of course. It is now said in Spanish, with the priest facing the people, with more congregational participation, and sometimes with a distinct Mexican flavor in music, vestments, and the like. These and many other changes came about through the Second Vatican Council's attempt to make Catholicism more culturally and personally relevant worldwide. But many, many Mexican Catholics, especially men, seldom go to Mass.

A statue of the Virgin of Remedies (La Virgen de los Remedios) came to Mexico with Cortés and disappeared during La Noche Triste, the Spanish soldiers' disastrous retreat from Mexico City. The tiny figure was found later by an Indian and was restored to her place as the protector of Mexico City. This Virgin was carried on the banners of the Royalist forces during the War of Independence and has often been invoked in the aid of conservative causes.

It isn't that people are against the Church and its official teachings. Rather, traditional folk or popular Catholicism, with its daily and seasonal rituals, its multitude of saints upon whom one may call, and its means of coping with the results of human nastiness, provides many working-class people with what they feel they need. Many of the concerns of the contemporary Church may seem quite irrelevant to the poor, who must concentrate on making it through to the next day, the next week, the next year. Mexican folk Catholicism, with its decidedly pragmatic nature and its wealth of potential heavenly helpers, serves this purpose.

Folk Saints of the Borderlands

A sort of devout anticlericism seems to be a major characteristic of popular, working-class Mexican Catholicism. In the first years of the Conquest, missionary priests were foreigners, totally alien to the communities in which they worked. Traditionally, the Mexican clergy, and especially the hierarchy, saw themselves as tied by interest and class identity to the privileged few. The following story may serve to illustrate this point: The Archbishop of Morelia gave a Christmastime *posada* celebration at some point in the late nineteenth century. All of the *piñatas* were filled with the black, sticky fruit of the *zapote* tree. The garments of the men, women, and children who scrambled for the "prizes" when the piñata was broken were covered with stains. Even though the archbishop's guests might not have been from the poorest classes, such a prank argues a degree of insensitivity on the part of that particular clergyman. During the nineteenth and early twentieth centuries, the Church practice was to charge for performance of such sacraments as weddings. This strongly affected the rural and urban poor, who often had no way of raising the fees necessary to pay for the various sacraments with which the Church marks an individual's life cycle.

Even today, many priests in Mexico still seem to be people set apart from the struggles of daily life. In rural Sonora, for instance, the priest is usually from outside the village and may stay only a few years in any given place. He is separated from the bulk of his parishioners by education, often by class, and by the assurance that, come what may, he will not starve. He has the power to forbid age-old religious fiestas and other customs, and frequently has exercised this power. Priests in Mexico often look upon the churches where they are assigned, along with their contents, as being theirs to dispose of as they see fit. This has sometimes resulted in the

> 🜨 **Las Posadas** or **"The Lodgings"** consists of a series of nine processions held all over Mexico just before Christmas. It commemorates Joseph and Mary's search for shelter in Bethlehem. The final procession usually ends with the breaking of a piñata—a large clay pot or papier-mâché container decorated with cut, colored paper and filled with candies and other good things.

alteration or removal through sale or gift of images that were of great local spiritual and sentimental importance.

For many poor Catholics, the priest and his official Church views are more or less irrelevant to their daily lives. Attendance at Mass is rare, except for such life-cycle rituals as baptism, marriage, and burial. When they enter the church building, it may well be in order to pray before the image of a particular saint, rather than to attend daily Mass. I have heard Anglo-American priests stationed at the Baroque Colonial church of San Xavier del Bac in Arizona complain that supplicants walk into church, cross in front of the altar, light candles and pray before a favorite image, and leave, all while Mass is going on!

This book examines just one aspect of this traditional, highly pragmatic Mexican folk Catholicism. Moreover, it is concerned with the folk Catholicism of a specific, unique region—the borderlands of the United States and Mexico. It is now time briefly to examine this setting.

THE BORDER

The United States/Mexico border stretches from the Gulf of Mexico all the way to the Pacific Ocean. It is a line, of course, that can be traced both on a map and on the ground, where it takes the form of a physical barrier of some sort. The eastern portion of the border is a river, called the Río Bravo in Mexico and the Rio Grande in Texas. Increasingly, the rest of the border consists of a metal wall, erected by the United States government; but in more rural, desert areas it can be as flimsy as a three-strand barbed-wire fence. River, wall, and fence serve as notices to those on either side that they should not cross over to the other country without going through certain formalities concerning both their persons and their property. One aspect of the border, then, is that it serves as a barrier, albeit a porous one, between two sovereign nations.

Folk Saints of the Borderlands

But the border is also a magnet, because the two nations are very different from each other, with different needs, problems, and opportunities. Machinery and appliances manufactured in the United States are often cheaper and more available than those manufactured in Mexico, for instance, so an active import trade, both legal and illegal, has existed for years. Certain drugs are illegal in the United States, so there exist powerful and widespread organizations to grow or create those drugs in Mexico and smuggle them into the United States. Labor is plentiful and jobs scarce in Mexico, while certain kinds of workers are in relatively short supply in the United States. Therefore thousands of men, women, and children cross the border each year, headed north to the United States, in search of employment and a better life. Mexico offers cultural and recreational attractions that are enjoyed by thousands of American tourists. All these goods and people must cross the border, legally or otherwise.

Therefore the border is a place of tension. Some of these tensions are those one would expect in a zone dividing a very wealthy and comparatively sparsely populated country from a poor and crowded one. Some are the result of the coming together of two very different cultures and languages—two sets of rules for living, if you will. Some are connected with the hazards of transporting goods illegally across the border—and those goods include immigrants. Not only does the undocumented immigrant have to cross the border without detection, he or she must continue to escape detection and deportation once in the United States. It is possible to legalize one's status, of course, but this process is itself a risky and often arduous one, involving interaction with often-incomprehensible laws and bureaucracy.

But the border is not just a line—it is a cultural zone all its own. Traces of the language and culture of each land can be found long after one has crossed the line and gone into the other country. Visitors to Mexico complain that the border cities of Tijuana, Baja California, and Nogales, Sonora, for example, are not the "real Mexico." Neither, for that matter, are Brownsville and

Laredo, Texas, the "real United States." Each is a border city, with an amalgam of customs, practices, traditions, and problems unique to the border.

Because the border runs through territory that was part of Mexico—and occupied by Mexican citizens—long before it became part of the United States in the nineteenth century, a sizeable, long-standing Mexican population lives on the U.S. side of the border. This population has grown steadily over the years, as political and economic conditions make emigration to the United States desirable for Mexicans. But even those men and women of Mexican descent and culture whose families have been United States citizens since the mid-nineteenth century have not necessarily lived here as equal social, economic, or political partners with Anglo-Americans. This is not the place to go into the causes for this inequality, but suffice it to say that prejudices toward Spanish-speaking Catholics have lurked in English-derived Protestant culture since the sixteenth century. These prejudices and inequalities, added to the rapidly increasing rate of immigration from Mexico, increase the tensions of life on the border.

These increased tensions are signaled in a number of ways. The agitation for and modified passage of "English only" laws, restricting the use of Spanish in schools and other state-sponsored settings, is one indicator. A high rate of school dropouts among Mexican-American students is another indication that things are not well in this region. Increased immigration enforcement in urban and relatively controllable areas has turned the southwestern Arizona desert into a killing field where scores of people die each year due to heat and dehydration.

All is not well on the Mexican side of this binational zone, either. The institution of large numbers of *maquiladoras,* assembly plants in Mexico's border zone where cheap labor is available and the finished product can be shipped duty-free back to the United States, has brought with it a huge population influx. This in turn has created a number of problems, including the murders of dozens of young women in Ciudad Juárez in the 1990s. The drug trade has brought increased lawlessness to the border, as *mafiosos* attempt to smuggle drugs in one direction and money in the other. It would not be inaccurate to say that the drug trade has affected virtually everyone on both sides of the border in some way or another.

The border seems always to have been a violent place. From Henry Alexander Crabb's filibustering expedition to Caborca, Sonora, in 1857, to Juan Nepumuceno Cortina's 1859 occupation of Brownsville, Texas, to Pancho Villa's 1916 raid on Columbus, New Mexico, the entire length of the border has seen more than its share of bloodshed. The drug-related killings of the present simply continue this pattern. The *corridos*—Mexican narrative folk ballads—of the Texas border region take violence as a major theme, as do today's *narcocorridos* (story songs celebrating the exploits of Mexico's drug runners and dealers).

In this border country, a land of conflict, danger, opportunities, and dramatically uneven distribution of wealth, we find the setting for this book. More specifically, the book deals with some aspects of the folk religion followed by men and women of Mexican heritage—Mexicanos, Chicanos, and Mexican Americans—who live or work in the border zone, on both sides of the line. Some of these individuals are permanent residents; others come to the border as would-be immigrants or participants in the drug trade. All are in one way or another border people, living or working in a region of several cultures and languages, where risks and rewards alike can run high.

The Folk Saints

Most specifically, this book deals with a number of individuals now deceased and in one way or another venerated and called on for help by border folks. None of them is likely ever to qualify as a saint within the formal structure of the Catholic Church. Three were regarded by the poor and powerless of their regions as saints in their lifetimes, three were not. They include one convicted murderer, two bandits, and three faith healers. Few are popular the length and breadth of the border; each has his or her area of influence. Some appear to be growing in importance; one is decidedly on the wane.

Here they are, from west to east. Juan Soldado was a young soldier executed in the 1930s for a crime his followers claim he did not commit, and who is buried in a cemetery in Tijuana, Baja California. Jesús Malverde was a Sinaloan stage robber who may or may not have existed and whose chapel in Culiacán, Sinaloa, attracts thousands of visitors, including many people involved in the drug trade. He is often referred to as *el santo de los narcotraficantes* ("the saint of the drug dealers"), although many people not engaged in that world call on him for help as well. Teresa Urrea, or Santa Teresita—a young Sonoran woman with remarkable healing powers—was expelled from Mexico for subversive activities in 1892. She died in 1906 in Clifton, Arizona. Pancho Villa went from being a bandit to being an important general in the Mexican Revolution and was then defeated by government forces in the civil war that followed. He was murdered in Parral, Chihuahua, in 1923. Don Pedrito Jaramillo was an elderly faith healer who achieved great fame for his numerous cures and his generosity in south Texas around the turn of the nineteenth century. His grave near Falfurrias, Texas, is both a pilgrimage shrine and a state historical landmark. José Fidencio Constantino Síntora was another faith healer who achieved international fame in the 1920s and 30s. His shrine stands where he worked his cures, in the tiny settlement of Espinazo, Nuevo León. His followers effect cures by channeling his spirit in special ceremonies and allowing him to act through them. Followers of El Niño Fidencio are called *Fidencistas;* the mediums who channel him are *materias* or *cajones.*

None of these individuals, as I said, is likely ever to be considered for sainthood by the institutional Catholic Church. However, this is of no importance to their followers, who pray to them, channel them, visit their shrines, buy devotional representations of them, and believe themselves to have been helped by them. These devotions exist within the behavior patterns of Catholicism, although channeling the spirits of the dead is in fact condemned by the Church. However, the devotions are totally outside the formal structure of the Church. They are, in fact, folk devotions in the simplest sense: they were created by a certain group of people in order to fill needs felt by those same people. Outside their particular world, they are not only disapproved of, they are to a great extent unknown.

COMING TO THE SUBJECT

This book came about in the following manner. In the early 1990s I started to collect contemporary Mexican Catholic printed religious ephemera, starting in my hometown of Tucson, Arizona, and the nearby pilgrimage center of Magdalena, Sonora. Eventually this collection expanded to include English-language material from the United States, and even other countries, as these became available. One of my original motives was aesthetic: I knew that Mexican popular artists such as José Guadalupe Posada had created devotional images for mass sale, and I was curious to see what was "out there." Another motive was iconographic: I was curious as to how one distinguished between the many specific Christs and Virgins I was learning about: El Señor de Chalma, for instance, or El Señor del Sacromonte; or the Virgins of San Juan de los Lagos, Fátima, and los Rayos. (The answer, especially in the case of crucifixes, is that one often *doesn't* distinguish among them, unless the image is labeled.) I was also interested in visiting popular religious sites in Mexico, and this made a wonderful excuse to do so.

As the collection grew (and it numbers well over two thousand items now), I began to find cards with prayers addressed to some very unusual-sounding individuals. These included La Santísima Muerte (the Most Holy Death), El Ajo Macho (the Male Garlic), El Coyote, and even Jupiter Lucifer, Rey de los Demonios (Jupiter Lucifer, King of the Demons). These images and incantations brought me into contact with another side of Mexican folk Catholicism, an extension of the pragmatism I have already mentioned. It seems there are many powers surrounding this world, each with its specialized interests and abilities. If God and the saints are uninterested in a given need or project, perhaps there might be Someone Else who could help.

This was brought home to me through a narrative by a Sonoran mafioso, passed on to me through a third party. A very pious woman in his home village in Chihuahua had a violent, brutal son. He would beat her for any reason—even if he did not like the way she pressed his shirts. She prayed to God and the Virgin to change his heart, but to no avail. Finally she prayed for help to the Devil. That night he beat her once more and rode on his way to a fiesta. As he rode through a *barranca,* a round, hairy object dropped off the cliff, knocked him out of the saddle and beat him so badly he ended up in the hospital. When he got out, his mother explained to him just what had happened. He beat her again, and was himself badly beaten in turn. When he recovered this time he left her a note to the effect that he was incurably evil and was going away, never to see her again. The point in passing this story on to me (and it was sent to me in response to a question I had asked concerning some of the more disturbing prayer cards I had been acquiring) seems to be this: A person is surrounded by powers and forces of all sorts. One needs ask for help where the help is likely to be effective.

Along with these cards, some of which must be described as containing charms and spells rather than prayers, were prayers addressed to people I did not recognize as saints within the boundaries of the Catholic Church. Juan Soldado was one of these; so were Pancho Villa and Jesús Malverde. At about that time, Richard Morales and I paid the visit to the Juan Soldado Chapel described at the start of this chapter. This piqued my curiosity even more, and I started actively pursuing information about these individuals who appeared to function like saints. I collected more prayer cards and visited various shrines and chapels throughout the border country. I asked a lot of questions of many people. This book is the result of that quest—the interim result, that is, as human culture changes constantly, and any work of this kind can only be a progress report on what the researcher has found so far and a slice of the reality of a specific period of time.

A hand-tinted, photographic holy card of Juan Soldado.

CHAPTER 2

JUAN SOLDADO

A Victim Who Won't Stay Down

Juan Soldado is considered a spirit rather than a saint by many of his devotees, but like a saint, he is believed to intercede with God on behalf of his friends. Little is known, or at least told, of his life except the manner of its ending—a supposedly unjust military execution. Like so many poor people before and after him, he was simply in the wrong place at the wrong time, with no means of defending himself. One detail about Juan Soldado, however, sets him apart from other, similar figures. He is a historical character who appears in the published record. Most importantly, there exists an image believed to be of him.

This photograph shows a very young man, smooth of face, in the uniform of a Mexican army private of the 1930s. He stands somewhat casually, with his right hand resting on a table. A small crucifix stands on the table. I have been told that rather than indicating a special religiosity on the part of this particular individual, this was a standard pose of the time for young men who had just joined the army and were leaving home.

This photograph is reproduced on printed prayers to Juan Soldado and on votive candles. The image is also copied, usually without the accompanying table and crucifix, for full-length cast-plaster statues. In the case of the statues, the uniform is painted green. More common than the full-length statues, however, are busts, showing the same peaked, visored cap as the photograph. This image appears over and over again, and prayer cards to Juan Soldado bearing the full-length image may be purchased at religious-articles stalls in Baja California and Sonora.

Juan Soldado also has a name—Juan Castillo Morales—and a death date—February 17, 1938. Here is the story of his death as it appears in written history.

THE HISTORICAL RECORD

Tijuana, Baja California, was in a state of considerable turmoil in January 1938. The border town had fared well as long as Prohibition was in force in the United States. Many Californians, among them such Hollywood luminaries as Rita Hayworth, Orson Welles, Mickey Rooney, Charles Chaplin, and Gloria Swanson, would cross the border for the sort of good times no longer available in the United States. Casinos, horse races, and other activities were booming, and times were high in Tijuana. In fact, the city has been described as a "regulated vice haven catering to foreigners." But following the repeal of Prohibition in 1933, the expulsion of thousands of Mexican workers from California during the Depression, and the 1935 decree of President Lázaro Cárdenas prohibiting games of chance, things changed drastically for the worse. The lure of liquor and gambling no longer called Americans across the border, and Tijuana was flooded with unemployed workers. Mass unemployment, intense rivalry between various labor organizations, and the sharp drop in the flow of money from the United States all combined to create an extremely volatile situation. The spark was set to the tinder in February of 1938.

On the afternoon of February 13, an eight-year-old girl named Olga Camacho was reported missing to the local police department. Her body was found next morning, and it appeared that she had been raped and murdered. A soldier named Juan Castillo Morales was arrested the same day and accused of the crime. Juan Castillo (according to traditional Mexican usage, the mother's family name is written last, after that of the father) was a twenty-four-year-old recruit—some say he was from Jalisco— reportedly found with blood on his clothes. He was taken to the Tijuana jail and locked up. A lynch mob gathered from the already angry populace, incited apparently by labor leaders. Early in the morning of February 15, they managed to burn both the police headquarters and the *palacio municipal*. Firemen attempting to reach the scene were unable to do so, as rioters lay down in front of the fire trucks, pulled wires from their motors, and slashed their tires. Help from the San Diego fire department did not arrive in time to save either building. Several people were reported wounded and one killed in the riot, and many individuals were jailed.

The military authorities, seeing the civil authorities more or less in a state of paralysis, took over and subjected Juan Castillo to a military tribunal. He was sentenced to death and, at 8 a.m. on February 17, taken to the cemetery. Here he was shot in the presence of a number of onlookers, probably after having dug his own grave. The phrase I've heard used to describe this kind of execution in Mexico is *"aplicaron la ley fuga"*—"they applied the law of flight." In other words, the individual concerned was "shot while trying to escape"—an escape that was never a real possibility.

The next day, an older woman—some say it was his mother—placed a stone on Juan Castillo's death site and left a sign asking passersby to place a stone there and pray an "Our Father." With this action, Juan Castillo Morales seems to have started on his transformation from a hated murderer to a martyred folk saint.

Folk Saints of the Borderlands

The Legends

Perhaps the best way to describe this journey is to relate the legend of Juan Soldado as it is told by those who believe in him. ("Juan Soldado" literally means "John Soldier," but the phrase has much the same strength as "G.I. Joe" in English). I first heard Juan's story on that December day in 1982 when, as I told in our first chapter, Richard Morales and I parked our car by a roadside chapel and walked up a dirt road to ask questions about this figure who was completely new to us. The lady who greeted us at the ranch house at the end of the road told us this version of his story:

Juan Soldado is *un alma* (a soul), not a *santo*. He was a *soldado raso*, or army private, in Tijuana, Baja California Norte. His *capitán* raped and murdered an eight-year-old girl who had come to the garrison with food or laundry or something. The captain accused Juan of the crime, and then applied la ley fuga on him. Juan began appearing to the captain and to the captain's *novia* or sweetheart. The captain finally admitted his own guilt and died, and Juan began to respond to the needs of those who prayed for the repose of his soul. A chapel was eventually built to Juan in the cemetery in Tijuana where he was buried.

The woman had first heard of Juan in Hermosillo, the capital of Sonora, some two hours' drive to the south. She had asked him to help cure her sick daughter, and the daughter got better. Later Juan assisted the lady's son, who was in jail. The mother then built the chapel we had just visited. She told us of other miracles and then remarked that most of the local Catholic clergy approved of Juan (whom she referred to as *"mi Juanito"*). One priest, however, did not approve and said that the devotion to Juan was in fact the devil's work. That priest was dying in Tucson even as we spoke, she told us.

Several of the themes of this narrative were to become familiar as I learned more about Juan Soldado and his devotees. Most of the people who knew about Juan told much the same story. The rank of the guilty officer would change from captain to sergeant to major to general, and some details would be added. For instance I was later told that Juan's sergeant, who had actually committed the murder, told Juan to go clean up a mess near the garrison. Blood on Juan's clothes resulting from this order was used as evidence against him. I was also told that Juan derived his powers from God and, like Jesus, he had been falsely accused and killed by those in authority. He has now been judged by God and found innocent.

But the general outline of the story remains the same in every believer's narrative that I have heard. There is the rape and murder of a young girl, the false accusation by a guilty superior officer, the subsequent execution, and the later confession on the part of the officer followed by miracles performed by Juan Soldado. Consistent as well are the themes of the narrator's being told about Juan in an hour of need, the answered prayer, and the subsequent act of gratitude. Even the opposition by the Catholic clergy seems to be a constant theme.

Only occasionally does a devotee have something to say about Juan's life. When historian Paul Vanderwood visited Juan's shrine on June 24, 2000, he collected two reminiscences of Juan Castillo. One woman said that when she was six she had been given a *paleta* or ice cream bar by Juan, who used to distribute sweets to children near the military post. Another woman told of how Juan taught neighborhood youngsters how to play sports. These glimpses seem to establish Juan Castillo as a kind person, albeit one who was consistently (and perhaps ominously) interested in children.

THE CEMETERY

Juan Soldado's traditional grave and death sites are in Panteón Jardín Número Uno (meaning "Garden Number One Cemetery") in Tijuana. The death site is at the rear of the upward-sloping cemetery, near a cliff. It is a logical place for an execution by firing squad, as any bullets missing their intended target can spend themselves harmlessly in the cliff. The other site, which has had a chapel at least since 1983, lies fairly close to the front gate of the cemetery, on fairly level ground, adjacent to what appears to be Juan's grave. In May 1983, on the first of my two visits, two-wheeled pushcarts stood in the street in front of the cemetery, one on either side of the gate. Snack food, drinks, and Juan Soldado pictures, printed prayers, flowers, and candles were for sale in and beside these carts. The grave site was easily accessible from the main path through the cemetery. It was surrounded by a blue picket fence. A three-foot cross cast of composition material stood at the head of the grave. A crucified Christ was suspended within a hollow in the center of the cross. Two statues depicting the Sacred Heart of Jesus stood next to the cross, as did several large sheaves of cut flowers. Several ex-voto plaques lay on the grave slab or leaned against the cross. To the left of this fenced enclosure stood a small, square chapel with a front porch slightly longer than the chapel itself. The chapel was painted light blue, as were the posts supporting the roof of the porch. A fili-gree ironwork cross stood on the roof of the chapel, directly over the door. To its left stood a bust of Juan Soldado surrounded by the remains of a wreath and to its right, an empty *nicho* (a niche, usually holding religious images). The chapel roof was littered with apparently discarded objects, including sev-eral cardboard model houses.

All four exterior walls of the chapel were hung with ex-voto plaques. These were mostly rectangular and averaged perhaps a foot high by sixteen inches wide. Occasionally I would notice a more striking offering. Against the north wall of the chapel leaned a seven-foot-high cross, made of four coils of heavy black automobile spring. In the center of the cross were a black wheel rim and a white hubcap. On the hubcap was painted

F.A.M.

1-2-25—X-29-78

A

JUAN-SOLDADO

A string of colored plastic pennants hung from the roofline of the porch. A clear path to the chapel door ran down the center of the porch, but both sides were filled with sheaves of cut flowers, many of which were in inexpensive vases. Many of these vases bore engraved dedicatory inscriptions. A typical one read GRACIAS JUAN SOLDADO POR EL MILAGRO CONCEDIDO, followed by the initials of the grateful petitioner. This phrase, which translates into English as "Thanks, Juan Soldado, for the miracle granted," appears over and over again on plaques at the site. The petitioner's name or initials are invariably given.

The interior of the chapel was filled with votive offerings. A spiral metal candleholder about three feet high with several squat votive candles on it stood between the door and the altar, which occupied the rear wall. At least three busts of Juan Soldado, all from different molds, stood on the altar table, along with other religious statues including the Sacred Heart of Jesus, the Virgin Mary, and the Holy Family. Two of the busts of Juan Soldado were so hung with photographs of petitioners as to obscure all save the faces of the statues. Candles, photographs, ex-voto plaques, and floral offerings took up most of the available wall and altar space. Considering that, with few exceptions, each of these objects was a separate offering from a different petitioner, they represent a large number indeed of miracles requested and granted.

The execution site, at the upper end of the sloping cemetery, right against a cliff face, was enclosed in a roofless brick room. Inside the room lay a rectangular, grave-sized rock pile enclosed in a frame made of one-by-six boards. At the head of the pile stood several crosses, some of wood and some of metal. At least one of each material was marked "Juan Castillo Morales." Offerings of real and artificial flowers lay on and near the rock pile, and several ex-votos rested against the rear wall of the enclosure. Also against the rear wall hung pictures of Nuestra Señora de San Juan de los Lagos and El Santo Niño de Atocha.

Both the chapel and the death site had changed considerably by the time of my second visit in 1998. The wooden supports of the porch had been replaced by arches painted to look like bright red bricks. On the roof of the porch stood a large white wooden sign containing the same standard prayer to Juan Soldado that appears on his prayer cards. An empty nicho stood at the center front of the chapel roof. The porch was still lined with ex-votos, flowers, and other offerings. These latter included a free-standing nicho of cast marble some three feet high, containing a white marble bust of Juan Soldado and marked with the year 1966. The flowers were fresh, most likely purchased at one of the carts outside the cemetery.

Inside the chapel, the spiral candleholder was no longer in evidence. On the altar stood three busts of Juan Soldado, the center one in a glass case. Each bust seemed to have been made with a different mold. I saw a tray for candles in front of the altar, and ex-votos and passport-sized photographs of individuals, mostly men, attached to the walls behind it. There were perhaps fifty ex-voto plaques inside the chapel.

The execution site had changed dramatically. A woman from California had reportedly financed the construction of a chapel. The building was gable-roofed, with stained glass in the triangle over the door. The rock pile and the crosses had disappeared. A large photograph of Juan Soldado hung on the rear wall of the chapel, along with several ex-votos, above a central offering of flowers and candles against the wall. I noticed at least one ex-voto that I had seen at the site in 1983. Several other ex-votos hung on the side walls, which in addition were covered with what I can only call devotional graffiti. Brief messages of thanks to Juan appeared in felt-tipped pen on both

⁂ **Our Lady of San Juan de los Lagos** has been venerated in San Juan de los Lagos, Jalisco, since 1623, when a small image of the Virgin was instrumental in bringing back to life a girl who had fallen on knives during a trapeze act. She is venerated over much of northern Mexico and along the border.

⁂ The **Holy Child of Atocha (El Santo Niño de Atocha)** is the young Christ Child as venerated in the mining community of Plateros, Zacatecas. He is patron of miners and prisoners, and is also believed to take special care of little boys.

Juan Soldado's execution site in the Panteón Jardín Número Uno, as seen in May 1983.

side walls, but not on the front wall, which was apparently left free for more formal offerings.

I have been referring confidently to the "grave site" and the "death site." It should be noted, however, that not all visitors to Juan's grave share these definitions. Several people we spoke with were unsure of exactly where Juan Castillo was buried. Some believe he may well be buried at the site of his execution, and the lower chapel may simply be a convenience for those who are too old or infirm to climb up to the far edge of the cemetery.

THE MIRACLES

There is no doubt that many people have found—and continue to find— Juan Soldado to be an effective provider of help. In our 1998 visit to the site, we counted about 150 ex-voto plaques on the outside of the chapel, another fifty within it, and thirty more, plus devotional graffiti, at the chapel recently built at Juan's reputed death site.

The texts of the ex-votos are statements of thanks, followed by the name or initials of the petitioner. Some are dated as well. Examples that follow give the Spanish text exactly as it appears on the plaque, but I've added standard punctuation to the English text. I have omitted names as being unnecessary and intrusive. Most of the texts refer to the miracles in general terms only.

GRACIAS JUAN SOLDADO POR EL MILAGRO CONCEDIDO. 1964. (Thanks, Juan Soldado, for the miracle granted.)

Or, a bit more elaborately: 1959 INFINITAS GRACIAS TE DOY JUAN SOLDADO POR EL MILAGRO QUE ME CONCEDISTES. (I give you infinite thanks, Juan Soldado, for the miracle that you have granted me.)

A few are more specific: TE DOY GRACIAS JUAN SOLDADO POR HABERME AYUDADO EN LOS MOMENTOS MAS DIFICILES DE MI VIDA. (I give you thanks, Juan Soldado, for having helped me in the most difficult moments of my life.)

BENDITO SEAS JUAN SOLDADO POR HABERME SALVADO A MI HIJI-TA. GRACIAS. (May you be blessed, Juan Soldado, for having saved my little daughter. Thanks.)

JUAN SOLDADO GRACIAS POR ALIVIARME DE LOS NERVIOS POR LOS QUE SUFRI TANTOS AÑOS. (Juan Soldado, thank you for having cured the nerves that I suffered for so many years.)

GRACIAS JUAN SOLDADO POR HABERME CONCEDIDO LA EMI-GRACIÓN. (Thanks, Juan Soldado, for having granted me emigration.)

GRACIAS JUAN SOLDADO POR INTERCEDER POR MI HIJO _____ YA QUE POR TU CONDUCTO DIOS AYUDABA MI HIJO A TERMINAR SUS ESTUDIOS. (Thank you, Juan Soldado, for interceding on behalf of my son ____, because through your intercession God helped my son finish his studies.)

1950 INFINITAS GRACIAS TE DOY JUAN SOLDADO POR HABERME CONCEDIDO EL MILAGRO DE SALVARME DE LA PRISION TAN GRANDE QUE SE ME ESPERABA QUE DIOS TE TENGA EN SU SANTO REYNO POR HABERME CONCEDIDO ESTE MILAGRO. (I give you infinite thanks, Juan Soldado, for having granted me the miracle of saving me from the very big prison that awaited me. I hope that God has you in His holy kingdom for having granted me this miracle.)

This last ex-voto is in the form of a large composition cross with a central square on which the inscription appears. It stands at Juan Soldado's death site and appears in my 1983 photos of that area.

Although most of the nearly two hundred ex-votos take the form of plaques, a few take other forms. For instance, one small painting in the ramada depicts two doctors in white gowns operating on a patient. Juan Soldado's bust appears in the upper right-hand corner of the painting. In the upper left quadrant appears the following legend: _____ AGRADECE A JUAN SOLDADO POR SACARLA ADELANTE EN SU OPERACIÓN. GRACIAS. (_____ thanks Juan Soldado for having brought her out from her operation. Thanks.)

Another picture contains a pencil sketch of a young man holding a tiny baby. The legend reads JUAN SOLDADO. EN TUS MANOS LES PONGO/GUIALOS POR UN BUEN CAMINO Y DONDE QUIERA QUE ESTEN PROTEGELOS SON LOS SUPLICOS DE UNA ESPOSA ABILEGADA. (Juan Soldado. In your hands I place them. Guide them on a good road and protect them wherever they may be. These are the wishes of a grateful wife.) The sketch demonstrates considerable skill and talent and seems to have been copied from a photograph. The whole effect is deeply moving.

A third drawing shows a bearded Christ placing a rosary around Juan Soldado's neck. The legend in the lower right-hand corner reads GRACIAS JUAN SOLDADITO POR LOS MILAGROS QUE ILUMINADOS POR DIOS ME CONCIDISTE. 21-DIC.-91 (Thanks, little Juan Soldado, for the miracles that, enlightened by God, you granted me. Dec. 21, 1991).

17 de Febrero de 1938

ORACION

A LA ANIMA SOLA DE

JUAN SOLDADO

All depictions of Juan Soldado seem to be taken from this photograph.

I visited Panteón Jardín Número Uno in July 1998 for approximately 2½ hours on each of two consecutive days. During those visits devotees of Juan Soldado constantly came and went at the lower chapel, with a few going to the death site as well. Each day, we observed more than thirty people visiting the sites. Some of these individuals were happy to talk about their relationships with Juan. Two young mothers had come to pray for the health of their respective babies. Three men from Santa Ana, California, came to thank Juan for assisting with the immigration papers of one of the men.

One man had lost his wallet for the second time. It had his immigration papers in it. Rather than go through the hassle of getting his papers replaced again, he prayed to Juan Soldado and promised to visit the shrine if he found the wallet. He and his wife turned their house upside down, but the wallet could not be found. He personally felt he had left it on the table, but it was simply not there. Then his wife went to the store, and when she opened her purse to pay for her purchases, there was the wallet! This was that man's visit of thanksgiving, in fulfillment of his promise to Juan Soldado.

Another woman had promised to clean the chapel if her petition were granted. It was, and she was there working for several hours along with a man she had hired for the purpose. She had also promised and said a Rosary. She said she had had two petitions granted. The first one was curious. She wondered how it would feel to win the lottery, so she asked Juan Soldado to help her do so. She named a relatively small sum she wanted to win—$10,000. She bought a ticket, scratched it, and discovered that she had indeed won

$10,000. She then went to a priest and confessed what she had done. When he scolded her for praying to Juan Soldado, she told him: "I'm going to thank Juan Soldado, because it was through him, and not you, that I won the money!" She didn't describe her second petition.

She also explained a custom involving the many little stones sitting inside the chapel near the candles. You make a petition, she told us, and take a stone. When the petition is granted, you return the stone, and bring another stone to go with it. If a second petition is made, you take the original stone with you again. If that petition is granted, that stone is yours, and you keep it with you for the rest of your life. It can be in your purse or in your pocket, but it should always be with you.

JUAN SOLDADO & THE INSTITUTIONAL CHURCH

The theme of opposition by the Catholic Church came up in several conversations at the shrine. One person told us that there should be a big church on the site, but that the priests will not permit it. Others said that nobody knows what happens to the offerings of money left in the collection box and hinted that it might be taken and used by the official Church. (This contrasts with the situation at the shrine of Jesús Malverde in Culiacán, Sinaloa, where a self-appointed caretaker collects large sums of money and distributes them to the poor.) Some people said that a priest did say Mass at the shrine on June 24, El Día de San Juan (Saint John the Baptist's Day, and therefore, by extension, Juan Castillo's saint's day), but others felt this not to be the case. All did say, however, that this was a day of special activity, with constant coming and going of devotees, and with a steady stream of musicians who had been hired to sing *las mañanitas* to Juan (the Mexican equivalent of the American "Happy Birthday" song).

In one of the newspaper articles on Juan Soldado, Father Salvador Cisneros, rector of the Sacred Heart Seminary in downtown Tijuana, is

Folk Saints of the Borderlands

Statues of Juan Soldado, surrounded by St. Jude (with the medallion), the Virgin of Guadalupe, the Sacred Heart of Jesus, and the Holy Child of Atocha in the shop of sculptor Cruz Lopez, on Magdalena's main plaza. (July 1983)

quoted as saying that the Church looks on the cult of Juan Soldado as "something closer to a superstition, or a false gospel, than an authentic religious movement." He added that Juan's main miracle is helping people enter the United States illegally and that, although there is "no real evidence either way," the Church also doubts Juan Castillo's innocence.

Oddly enough, the woman proprietor of one of the *carretas* selling Juan Soldado photos and prayer cards at the cemetery gate shared these doubts. The "true story," according to her, is that he was guilty of raping and murdering the child. He had blood all over his uniform and literally was caught red-handed. Everything pointed to him as the true culprit, she said. *El pueblo*—the common people of Tijuana—turned against him and gave him la ley fuga. Olga was originally buried in the same cemetery as he was, but her family was upset at all the attention paid to her murderer and had her body moved to another cemetery. Juan Soldado's family is still in town, but refuses to be interviewed. To this day, this woman believes Juan Soldado was guilty and does not understand why he is venerated. Nevertheless, she sells Juan Soldado items at his shrine.

JUAN SOLDADO BEYOND TIJUANA

Although the major pilgrimage destination associated with Juan Soldado remains the Tijuana cemetery where he was killed and buried, I know of at least one other public chapel that was dedicated to him. This was on International Highway 15 in Sonora, just south of Magdalena—the place where I first encountered Juan. The chapel changed over the years since December 1982, when I first noticed it. As it stood in 2000 it was a one-room white building on the east side of the highway, surrounded on three sides by a portico supported by arches. Pilasters graced the supporting columns across the front of the chapel. A filigree iron cross stood over the door. Below it, in painted black letters shaded with light brown, was written LA CAPILLA DE JUAN SOLDADO. (Earlier signs were made of wood and variously read ANIMA.DEL.PURGATORIA JUAN SOLDADO and EL ANIMA DE JUAN SOLDADO.)

The chapel was equipped with a screen door, the upper third of it embellished with a white-painted filigree cross. A stepped altar occupied the head wall of the chapel. In the center of this altar stood a full-length, two-foot-high statue of Juan Soldado, leaning on a pedestal surmounted by a crucifix. Glass-enclosed candles clustered in front of him, while arrangements of brilliantly colored flowers filled the two steps on either side of him. On the white wall behind him and above his head was a print of the reclining San Francisco statue venerated in nearby Magdalena. It was flanked by pictures of the Virgin, in turn flanked by small bowls containing holy water. On one of the steps of the altar rested an ex-voto thanking Juan for a miracle involving the petitioner's son. This description applies to the chapel as I last saw it. By some time in late 2001 or early 2002, the chapel I had been visiting for almost twenty years had been razed to the ground. No traces of it remain visible from the highway.

Magdalena, being a pilgrimage center, has several stores stocking religious ephemera, and at least one of these stores usually carries Juan Soldado prayer cards. In the early 1980s I knew of at least one sculptor creating saints' images, who had several molds from which he cast statues and busts of Juan Soldado. I even saw a life-sized Juan Soldado statue in his display window on one occasion. I suspect that sales of these Juan Soldado keepsakes were helped by the presence of the chapel just a few kilometers down the road.

The owner of the chapel had heard of Juan from a sister who lived in Hermosillo, the capital of Sonora, several hours' drive south of her ranch. She had called upon him in time of need and had erected the chapel out of gratitude for a miracle granted her. A major east-west highway, International Highway 2, runs from Highway 15 west to Tijuana, which seems to be the logical route for the spread of this particular devotion. The pattern is a familiar one in folk Catholicism. One finds oneself in great need and hears of a saint or spirit by whom a friend or relative has been helped. One tries him or her out, and if the miracle is delivered, one passes the information on to one's own circle of friends.

> The reclining statue of Saint Francis Xavier has great regional importance in southern Arizona and northern Sonora and is the object of a huge annual pilgrimage. Thousands walk the sixty miles from the border at Nogales to Magdalena, Sonora, to make petitions or to pay vows. Curiously, the feast day on which the statue is venerated is not December 3 (the feast day of St. Francis Xavier in the Catholic calendar), but October 4—the Day of St. Francis of Assisi, a different saint altogether.

VICTIM INTERCESSORS

Juan Soldado's story—dying a violent death and being buried on the spot—and his following are not unique in the borderlands. Take, for example, Tucson's famous El Tiradito. The word means "the little thrown-away one" and applies both to the individual concerned and to his shrine. More than twenty legends concerning El Tiradito's origin are on file at the University of Arizona Library's Southwest Folklore Archives. All agree that one or more individuals met a sudden death and were buried where they fell. In most narratives, the dead person or persons were far from saintly—one popular story has a man catching his wife and his son-in-law in the midst of an affair and killing them on the spot. The site itself was moved to its present location in the late 1920s, after the original shrine was destroyed in a road-widening project. But the shrine remains, and it remains in constant use. You won't see ex-votos or offerings except candles, but I have seen candles burning at El Tiradito every time I have visited the site since the mid-1950s. People still call upon El Tiradito for help of all sorts, and apparently he is believed to deliver that help.

In the border town of Nogales, Sonora, are two similar figures. A soldier named Pedro Blanco was murdered one night, possibly in the 1920s, when he crossed an *arroyo,* or dry streambed, on his way home from a gambling game in which he had won heavily. And a woman named Tita Gómez was gathering wild onions on a hill south of Nogales when her boyfriend struck and killed her with a tire iron. Both Blanco and Gómez were buried where they fell. Each was believed at one time to grant petitions, and each was eventually moved to public cemeteries in Nogales. Today, Pedro Blanco rests in the Panteón Rosario, Nogales' oldest cemetery, while Tita Gómez occupies a plot in the huge Panteón Nacional. At neither grave have I found candles, ex-votos, milagros, or any other evidence that people still address petitions to these individuals, suggesting that their popularity has faded.

Three Mexican men are said to have been arrested for a serious crime soon after they got off the train in Benson, Arizona, possibly around 1900. Although innocent, they were speedily hanged without trial and buried just outside the Benson Cemetery. For years, I am told, people left ribbons and candles at a nearby mesquite tree. By the 1980s, tree, candles, and ribbons had all disappeared, as had most memories of the incident, if indeed it actually happened.

Near the old mission community of Oquitoa, Sonora, in the Altar Valley, stands the tiny chapel of El Chapo Charo. (Chapo is local Spanish for "shorty" and Charo is a standard nickname for "Rosario.") I have been told that El Chapo was a local man who "got involved in politics" early in the twentieth century and was taken by his enemies and given la ley fuga. He is said to be buried in nearby Átil, but so far I have been unable to elicit more details of his life. However, people have prayed to him for many years, and the present, fairly elaborate chapel was erected around 1990 by one particularly grateful family.

Farther to the south and east, people from the town of Opodepe found the body of an

The grave of Carlitos el Milagro (Carlitos Ángulo) in the Panteón Yañez in Hermosillo. (January 2003)

unidentified man out in the brush many years ago. For one reason or another, they could not load him into the available car, so he was dragged back to town and buried outside the cemetery, in unsanctified ground. (This might not have been unusual treatment of a totally unknown man in a Catholic community, especially before Vatican II.) He is known to this day as El Arrastradito ("the little one who has been dragged"), and locals ask his spirit for help in finding lost objects. His grave still lies in the brush across from the cemetery.

In the Panteón Yáñez in Hermosillo lies the grave of a boy named Carlos Ángulo F. (the "F." being the first letter of his mother's surname). Carlitos was killed at the age of about ten years, probably when an adobe wall fell on him. The date of his death is marked on his grave as being January 1, 1940. His grave is quite unusual—it consists of a small coffin standing upon open-work cast iron legs, the whole painted silver. At the foot of the casket is a sign: POR CARLITOS RUEGUE VD Y EL ESPIRITU DEL NIÑO LE AYUDARÁ (Pray for Carlitos and the little boy's spirit will help you). Offerings of cut flowers, teddy bears, and toy trucks adorned the tomb. We were told that the devotion is still quite active, and one young man told us that his father, a taxi driver, had been taking people to the grave site for some thirty-five years.

Finally, far to the east of all these sites, in Ojinaga, Chihuahua, across the border from Presidio, Texas, we find the shrine of El Difunto Leyva ("Leyva the dead man"). Nobody knows the dead man's first name, although there is some evidence that it might have been Juan. He was a man without family, who, sometime perhaps in the 1920s or 30s, was accused by a jealous husband. His accuser (who might have caught him in the act) burned him alive. As he died, Leyva raised his right arm and, pointing to heaven with one finger, said *"Al cabo allá está Dios"* ("God is there in the end"). His finger was the only part of him not totally consumed in the flames. It was kept in a glass container in the Difunto Leyva's chapel for many years, although it isn't there any more.

The chapel itself was in a state of considerable disrepair when I visited in March 2003. It stood in a cluster of small adobe houses, which had been partially demolished by the current owner, a local lawyer. He was delaying complete demolition of the area while a group of preservationists tried to raise money to purchase the site. The chapel itself was partially roofless. A tomb-like slab lay in the middle of the floor, and a stepped altar occupied the wall opposite the door. Several partially burned religious candles stood on the tomb and altar. The entire place, however, was very dirty and dusty, and the two remnants of wreaths on the floor looked as though they had been there for at least a year. Whatever ex-voto notes and offerings had been in the chapel were now stored in a local museum. My traveling companion Alfredo Gonzales and I got the strong impression during our visit to this site that the devotion is only tenuously maintained in Ojinaga.

I have taken to calling these individuals "victim intercessors," because they are believed to intercede on behalf of petitioners as saints do, yet nothing is known of their lives save for the fact that they died suddenly and even violently. Seldom is there any suggestion that those lives were in any way exemplary or even Christian. Occasionally, as in the case of Juan Soldado and also El Tiradito, one hears vague stories of how the individual was of a kind and benevolent nature. Such stories do not seem to be essential parts of the narrative pattern in either case. Some, like Juan Soldado, were victims of judicial murder, while others, like El Tiradito, were simply murdered. However they died, here they are, very much a part of the folk religion of the Western borderlands.

A Few Questions

This discussion of Juan Soldado leaves us with some serious unanswered questions. Foremost among them is the problem of just how and when Juan changed in the minds of the people of Tijuana. In his last days on earth he was presumed guilty, the object of the fury of an angry lynch mob. Today, more than sixty years later, he is a martyr figure—a powerless victim of the powerful, who has been vindicated after his death by God, the giver of *real* power. When did the switch occur? Was it connected with the rock pile, said to have been started immediately after his death? I have been told that no matter how many rocks were added to or taken away from that pile, it remained the same size. Or did the change in perception take place later on, when Tijuana's depression and tensions were moving into the past? Changes in popular opinion, especially in a strongly class-oriented society, are often almost impossible to trace, and while there may well be documentary evidence pointing toward an answer, I have not found it in my review of the secondary literature.

In a newspaper article, Anne-Marie O'Connor quotes Father Cisneros as emphasizing Juan's role in getting Mexican people across the United States border. Two of the three testimonials O'Connor quotes also deal with border issues. Yet a significant number of the ex-votos and personal interviews I have recorded deal with issues of health, of jail, and of education. Where does the truth lie? Do all or most of the *milagro concedido* plaques actually refer to immigration assistance? Are most of the photos on the altars in the Tijuana Cemetery connected with border crossings? Is Juan portrayed as a "one-issue" helper by outsiders, or is the perception of him as primarily a helper of immigrants an accurate one? A related question involves Juan's possible connection with people involved in the drug trade. Some of the ex-votos refer to jail experiences, and the woman we interviewed near Magdalena, Sonora, told of Juan helping free her son from prison. A doctor in Magdalena, Sonora, expressed the opinion that many of Juan's devotees were narcotraficantes. Are we simply experiencing an extension of the notion that Juan's followers must be somewhat disreputable outsiders? These questions and more remain in my mind.

One thing is certain, however. Juan Soldado is extremely popular as a supernatural helper along the Baja California/California border, and, if anything, his popularity seems to be increasing.

Portrait of Teresa Urrea.

CHAPTER 3

TERESITA

A Co-opted Healer

Gracias que ya hemos llegado
a este rancho a descansar
venid, venid pecadores
esta niña a visitar.

Thanks that we have now arrived
At this ranch to rest
Come, come, sinners
This girl child to visit.

–from a fragment of a poem found pasted inside the cover of a book on Mexican history published in 1883

If little or nothing is known of Juan Soldado up to the moment of his defining death, that is not the case with Teresita Urrea, La Santa de Cabora. Her life is well documented, and she played an important part in the history of late nineteenth-century Mexico. Books and articles have been written about her in both English and Spanish. However, her current status is a bit obscure. Is she simply a historical figure, or is some segment of the population using her assistance in some way to make their lives a little better? The latter seems more likely to be the case, although evidence remains scanty.

Folk Saints of the Borderlands

THE SONORAN YEARS

The child later to become known as Teresita Urrea, La Santa de Cabora, was born on October 15, 1873, on a ranch near the village of Ocoroni in the state of Sinaloa. Her mother was a local Tehueco Indian woman; her father, Don Tomás Urrea, was the son of a wealthy and powerful local family. Don Tomás acknowledged the illegitimate child as his daughter, and she was raised by her mother and an older aunt. She apparently grew to be a bit of a tomboy, riding horses and wrestling with the other children on the ranch. In 1880, when the child was seven, Don Tomás backed a candidate for governor of Sinaloa who defeated the candidate endorsed by president Porfirio Díaz, then just starting on what would be his long reign as Mexico's dictator. Díaz had the election proclaimed void and installed his own candidate in the governor's office. Tomás Urrea wisely feared reprisals and moved north to some family holdings in Sonora, near the old mining town of Álamos. The move involved livestock, household goods, family…and retainers. Among the latter were Teresa, her mother, and her aunt. They were settled on a subsidiary ranch at Aquihuiquichi, while most of the workers went on to create the main hacienda at nearby Cabora.

When Teresa was fifteen, her father sent for her to live with him at Cabora. There she worked with an older mestiza woman named Huila, who, in addition to her job of running the household, had skills as a *curandera* or healer. From Huila, Teresa learned to gather and use medicinal herbs and to apply traditional remedies. People noticed at this time that the younger girl had the ability to calm patients by touching them and looking into their eyes.

Then, at age sixteen or seventeen (in either 1889 or 1890), Teresa's life changed radically. Some traumatic experience—attempted rape has been suggested—caused her to go into a coma. According to tradition, she remained unconscious for more than twelve days and apparently died, only to "reawaken" as a wake was being held for her. She told Huila and others that she had spoken with the Virgin Mary and had been given much work to do. For months thereafter, she slipped in and out of trances. At the end of this time, she was a changed person.

For one thing, she could foretell the future and see things that were happening a long way off. She would "see" a family friend riding toward the hacienda; he would arrive several hours later. More importantly, she had great curing powers. She used the knowledge and herbal skills she had learned from Huila, who died shortly after Teresa's recovery—a death said to have been predicted by Teresa. In addition, she was possessed of personal healing powers. To effect some of her cures she used earth from Cabora that she moistened with her own saliva. She would often look deeply into the eyes of her patients and gently hold their hands in her own. She would also touch the afflicted parts of their bodies with her thumbs. According to all accounts, Teresa's eyes were large, luminous, and extremely compelling.

As word of her powers spread, people began to flock to the hacienda at Cabora in hopes of relief from their problems. She saw everyone who came to see her, and, by popular account, healed most of them. Some she could not heal, but, as she herself said, "If I fail to effect a cure on some, I never fail to greatly benefit them." I offer two anecdotes from this period of her life.

In 1890, she was visited by a man who had been unable to hear or speak for fourteen years. She told him, "You have eyes that do not see. You have ears that cannot hear." He heard these words, but very faintly. She then put cotton wads mixed with soil into his ears and his hearing gradually returned. In another case, she retired to her room to seek inspiration concerning a particular patient with an ulcerating sore on his leg. There she saw a phantom figure with a similar sore. Two small pieces of bone came out of the sore; when that happened, the shadow man threw away his crutch and walked. Teresa went back outside to her patient and washed his sore thoroughly. She then drew two similar bits of bone from his leg. The man left walking without a crutch, and, days later, seemed completely healed.

Folk Saints of the Borderlands

For about two years, Cabora became a place of pilgrimage. Teresita would see everyone she could, and by most accounts thousands arrived daily at the hacienda with petitions for this lovely young woman whom people were beginning to call a saint. This status she steadfastly denied, while agreeing that her power came from God and the Virgin. Whatever she was, her home was the focus of great attention. Sonorans of all classes, including Yaqui and Mayo Indians, arrived singly and in groups to seek her help. She never requested payment for her services, giving them freely to all who came. And come they did. At any given time, there may have been between a thousand and five thousand people camped at or near Cabora. Many were the poorest of the poor, although well-to-do Sonorenses also came to her when other means of relief failed. In a report to President Díaz, Governor of Sonora Lauro Carrillo referred to the goings-on at Cabora as a *romería*—a pilgrimage. In Mexico, that implies more than a number of people gathered at a religious destination. These people must be fed and entertained, and so it was at Cabora. Food sellers set up booths to feed the multitudes, and other *puestos* (booths) supplied various religious trinkets: prayer cards, pictures, scapulars, and medals with Teresita's image, as well as *milagros*—tiny ex-voto images in metal of various parts of the body. Musicians would play songs in honor of Teresita, along with popular songs and dance music of the time and place. Sellers of locally made mescal would have been there, as well as those who profited from the pilgrims in less savory ways: pickpockets, gamblers, and prostitutes. Such scenes can still be observed today at pilgrimage destinations all over Mexico. Inquirers from overseas and reporters from newspapers in Mexico and the United States also came to Cabora to see and hear. And there also came representatives of conservative Mexico's two most powerful forces: the Catholic Church and the federal government.

For Teresa did more than cure. She had a message as well, a message that bypassed the official intermediaries between humans and God that the Church provided. To the religious, she said that there was no need of priests to baptize or perform marriages. (These are two of the seven sacraments of the Catholic Church, along with the holy Eucharist, confirmation, penance, anointing of the sick, and holy orders. Baptism is the one sacrament that can be performed—in case of emergency—by lay people.) Father Manuel Castelo (also referred to in one source as Father Gustelúm), whose parish included many mountain villages just over the Chihuahua border to the east of Cabora, made it his business to visit Cabora and see what was going on. While there, he asked two nuns to test Teresita's supposed powers for him. While the young woman was in a trance, one of the nuns thrust a long hatpin into Teresita's leg. Then try as she might, she could not remove the pin. Awakening from the trance, Teresita withdrew the pin easily from her own calf. She showed no pain—and not a drop of blood. She then told the nuns to take the pin back to the priest who had sent them and tell him what they had seen. The repentant nuns, feeling themselves in the presence of a miracle, fell on their knees and begged forgiveness. Teresita calmly replied, "I do not perform miracles. Only God can do that." However, the Church hierarchy remained deeply suspicious of Teresita. She did not recognize their authority and was certainly upsetting the social and economic status quo—a condition the official hierarchy was deeply interested in preserving.

The federal government kept an eye on Cabora as well. Teresa was quoted as telling her followers to "live in peace and love one another; otherwise we offend the spirit of God." Such teachings struck, however indirectly, at the roots of the economic and social order of Porfirian Mexico, which was based upon the exploitation of the many by the few. Under his regime—a tightly controlled dictatorship—Porfirio Díaz kept in close touch with all of his governors, who had been personally selected by him. Governor Lauro Carrillo described the scene at Cabora in a personal letter to Díaz in January 1892. Despite the presence in great numbers of perpetually disaffected Yaqui and Mayo Indians, Carrillo apparently felt the situation not to contain an immediate menace to the state. However, matters were building to a head on several fronts.

REVOLT, EXILE & A NEW FRIEND

Despite the fact that Teresita apparently counseled her followers to love one another and did not encourage violence in any way, some communities heard her expressions of love and compassion and found in them words of encouragement to violent revolt. The first people to do so were native Mayo people, Cabora's near neighbors. Mayos were under great pressure to relinquish their rich farmlands to large-scale Mexican farming and had recently participated, along with Yaquis, in a war against the Mexican government. Mayo country was in a ferment, with several locally revered "living saints" prophesying the end times. In August 1890, a group of Mayos gathered at Jambiobampo, on a hill near Cabora, under the leadership of a young man who claimed to have consulted with Santa Teresita. They were awaiting a flood that would sweep the wicked from the face of the earth. Not surprisingly, Mexican intruders into traditional Mayo territory were numbered among the wicked. The Mexican military dispersed the crowd and arrested some sixty individuals. Other "living saints" kept appearing in villages all over Mayo country, and the situation became more and more tense. No active involvement on Teresita's part could be proven, although her name was on the lips of many of the discontented Indians. Finally, on May 15, 1892, around two hundred Mayos attacked the town of Navojoa, sacking it, and leaving several defenders dead and more wounded. The attackers were heard to cry "*Viva La Santa de Cabora*"—"Long Live the Saint of Cabora." Reprisals soon followed, and the army was able to track a number of the attackers in the direction of Cabora. In addition, two of the Mayo leaders indicated under questioning that their revolt had been inspired by La Santa de Cabora.

This was the end of Teresa's career in Sonora. On May 19, General Abraham Bandala and a strong detachment of troops arrived in Cabora and caught several of the rebels, tracking the rest into the sierra. Bandala then informed Don Tomás and his daughter that they must leave Cabora immediately and go into exile. This they did, while hundreds or possibly thousands of followers then at the hacienda passively watched and offered no resistance. The military escort took father and daughter through Yaqui country to Guaymas, in constant fear of Indian attack. From Guaymas, they proceeded by the newly constructed railroad to the border at Nogales. Teresita and her father crossed into the United States on July 5, 1892. A third person crossed into exile at about the same time: an engineer, Spiritist, and committed anti-Díaz revolutionary named Lauro Aguirre.

Born in mining country in Chihuahua and trained as a topographical survey engineer in Mexico's elite Colegio Militar, Aguirre found himself in the mid-1880s doing survey work in Sonora. Like any activity in Porfirian Mexico involving potentially valuable resources, land surveying was rife with possibilities for personal enrichment or, on the other hand, personal impoverishment while Don Porfirio's cronies lapped up the gravy. Aguirre experienced the latter fate, along with a large number of lawsuits, and he became an increasingly committed and vocal opponent of Porfirian rule. He was also an enthusiastic Spiritist. I shall now introduce this nineteenth-century religious movement, as well as its younger relative, Spiritualism, as we will encounter both systems over the course of this book.

SPIRITISM & SPIRITUALISM

Aguirre was a dedicated Spiritist, one of an increasing number of upper- and professional-class people in Mexico following to some degree the influential French occultist and writer Allan Kardek. Kardek, writing in the mid-nineteenth century, claimed that the spirits of the dead could maintain contact with those of the living through dreams. There were both good and bad spirits. Good spirits, or spirits of light, might look like angels, with wings, long hair, and robes, and helped the Spiritist combat the bad or dark spirits, who could be summoned by witches for the purpose of harming mankind. Out of Kardek's work arose the Spiritism movement. Spiritists believed that upon death one's spirit either stayed in this world for further purification or went to a spirit world, where it was possible for the spirit to improve sufficiently to be allowed to join God. Spirits in this world could communicate with those in the next. Mediums were individuals whose spirits were specially attuned for this task of communication. Furthermore, this world was slowly getting better, as so many nineteenth-century thinkers believed, and this progress would eventually lead to a sort of utopia under God.

Spiritism arrived in Mexico in the wake of the Emperor Maximilian, and, as I said, became especially popular among the upper and professional classes. Politically, Spiritists often tended towards a kind of liberalism, with a strong belief in the perfectibility of mankind. This goal would be accomplished with the help of the good spirits. One wealthy Spiritist—Francisco I. Madero, from an important land-owning family in Coahuila—eventually led the 1910 revolution that would overthrow President Díaz. He had previously served as commissioner for the First Mexican Spiritism Conference, held in Mexico City in 1906.

Some Spiritists denied the existence of God and considered Christ to have been simply an important medium and teacher. They were definitely outside the Catholic Church, and, in fact, the Church to this day considers the practice of Spiritism a "sin against religion." The official Church standpoint is that most mediumistic communications are frauds of some sort, and that no proven instance exists of communication between the living and the spirits of the dead. In the view of some churchmen, any spirits that might be communicating with humans are probably evil ones. Although Spiritism as a movement was most popular in the years

> ⚏ **Saint Martha (Santa Marta)** was the sister of Mary and of Lazarus, whom Jesus raised from the dead. Medieval legend has her traveling to southern France after Jesus' resurrection. There she rid the people of Provence of a dragon that was threatening them.

around the turn of the nineteenth century, many Spiritist assumptions and beliefs have gradually been adopted and adapted by working-class Mexicans and incorporated into a folk-Catholic framework.

Teresa's fame had spread rapidly among international Spiritism circles, and some of the more than one hundred letters she received daily at Cabora came from Spiritists in other parts of Mexico and even Europe. Closer to home, a small group of Spiritists in the nearby Sonoran mining town of Baroyeca paid a visit to Teresita and reported that she certainly was conversing with spirits and effecting cures. Although she never did conform with all aspects of Spiritist thinking (she continued to believe, for instance, that her powers came from God rather than spirits), she continued to fascinate the Spiritist community.

Spiritualism is a separate movement altogether, said to have originated in 1886 near the small town of Contreras to the south of Mexico City, with a priest named Roque Rojas. To this core, a Protestant component seems to have been added, especially in the north. The northern cities of Torreón and Monterrey are mentioned by anthropologist Isabel Kelly as being strong centers of Spiritualism. Kelly also emphasizes that Spiritualists tend to be urban working people of "modest social and economic position." Spiritualism seems to be mainly concerned with healing, performed by spirits who act through a medium who, for the purposes of the curing ceremony, "becomes" the spirit in question. Unlike Spiritists, Spiritualists function comfortably within the general framework of Catholicism, although their practices are not accepted by the official Church. They believe in God, and saints may be among the spirits whom they channel for their healing activities. When I was in the Lower Rio Grande Valley in 1998, I heard of a woman from Austin who came through the region on a regular basis, channeling Santa Marta. Although members of the Spiritism movement feature in the narratives of Teresita and, later on, El Niño Fidencio, the contemporary mediums who channel the spirits of the individuals featured in this book, as well as others, appear to be Spiritualists.

Folk Saints of the Borderlands

MORE VIOLENCE

En Cabora está la gracia	In Cabora is the grace
Y en Tomóchi está el poder	And in Tomochic the power
Qué gobiderno tan ingrato	What an ingrate government
Que no sabe comprender	That doesn't understand
Con el 11 y noveno batallón.	With the 11th and 9th Battalions.

–verse eleven of "El Corrido de Tomóchic," translated by Enrique Lamadrid

So here Teresita was in Nogales, Arizona, with her father, and in constant contact with Aguirre, a Spiritist who also believed in the violent overthrow of the Porfirian regime. For the next few years, Aguirre published a number of statements concerning Teresa, and it is difficult to tell when Teresa is speaking and when Aguirre is putting his Spiritism and political convictions in the healer's mouth.

In September of the same year—1892—violence erupted in Chihuahua. A number of the villagers of Tomochic in the rugged mountains of Chihuahua challenged the Church and the federal government by denying their obligation of obedience to either. They declared themselves to be acting in the name of God and Santa Teresita. They had gone to Cabora on an armed pilgrimage in December of 1891 but had failed to find their saint in residence. Even then, the government was deeply concerned with their rebellious attitudes and attempted unsuccessfully to halt their journey to and from Sonora. Unrest was spreading through the far northwest—unrest that belied Díaz' projected image of a Mexico filled with docile laborers. This image was vital to attracting foreign capital to the nation, a priority during the *Porfiriato* (the time Porfirio Díaz was in power). So President Díaz decided to act.

The details of the Tomochic rebellion have been presented thoroughly elsewhere and need not concern this narrative. Suffice it to say that, after successfully routing two detachments of Mexican soldiers sent against the village, the Tomochicos were besieged by forces far superior to their own and slaughtered to a man. Many were burned inside the church, which was set on fire by the federal troops, who shot every escapee who did not run toward them from the door. More were killed in the house of Cruz Chávez, leader of the revolt. Tomochic was a smoking ruin. The army first moved against Tomochic on September 2, 1892; the final slaughter took place on October 29.

Even though a "solution" had been found at Tomochic, violence in Teresa's name continued in the northwest of Mexico. In Ojinaga, the port of entry downstream from El Paso, a woman with a stone idol appeared and claimed to be in constant contact with God. When more than five hundred devotees gathered around La Santa, as they called her, the government moved to arrest her and confiscate the idol. She fled across the border, where she attracted yet more followers. The Mexican authorities arrested some followers in Mexico, and a rescue attempt on the part of yet more devotees ended in a bloody standoff. By the end of the incident, several people had been killed and the woman had vanished. Teresita claimed to have been one hundred miles away from Ojinaga at the time and not involved in any way.

But there were always the Yaquis, many of whom had a deep veneration for Teresita, and all of whom carried strong grudges against the Mexican government. Numbers of Yaquis were known to visit the Urrea home near the village of Tubac, Arizona, about twenty miles north of the Mexico border. Then, on August 12, 1896, a group of Yaquis attacked the customs house on the Mexican side of the border in Nogales, Sonora. They are said to have shouted such slogans as *"Viva La Santa de Cabora,"* *"Viva el poder de Dios,"* and *"Vivan los Tomochis."* A search of the corpses of the attackers revealed pictures of Teresita, scapulars, and copies of inflammatory articles written by Lauro Aguirre. Also found were unsigned letters, possibly also from Aguirre, urging the attack and promising assistance. Photographs were

Prayer card to Teresita, from the collections of the Arizona Historical Society, Tucson (used here with permission).

taken and peddled of Yaqui corpses lying in the street. Teresita again denied all involvement in or support for violence.

I mentioned holy cards bearing Teresita's picture. At least one such card still exists, in the collections of the Arizona Historical Society in Tucson. It shows a woman in a dark dress standing next to a cane-bottomed chair of sophisticated design, probably a photographer's studio prop. Her right hand rests on the chair back; in her left she holds a small sheet of paper. She wears a rosary around her neck, as well as a large crucifix. Two angels appear at her feet. The one at her right gestures in her direction, while the one at her left kneels, offering a crown. Two smaller angels hover over her head, holding a crown. More angel faces appear flanking her face, and rays of light emanate from her head. The angels are doubtless cut and pasted onto the original photograph from some other devotional card, probably to the Virgin in one of her manifestations. I have not identified a specific source. The card is captioned "TERECITA URREA. LA STA: NIÑA DE CABORA."

This card seems to be the source of a portrait created in Mexico City by the famous Mexican folk artist José Guadalupe Posada. His bust of Teresita resembles the holy card in all details. It is captioned "TERESITA URREA (LA SANTA DE CABORA), *a quien se atribuye por los periódicos gobiernistas una participación directa en los sucesos de Temóchic.*" ("Teresita Urrea, the saint of Cabora, to whom the government newspapers attribute a direct participation in the events at Tomochic.") Posada created several other engravings illustrating personalities and events connected with the battle at Tomochic. One such illustration, which poses more questions than it answers, is titled "*Corrido 'Santa de Cabora.'*" It depicts a young woman, tied to a T-shaped cross, being carried through a door by Mexican soldiers. She is accompanied by several men and women dressed as *peónes,* or peasants. The men are shouting and gesticulating; the women simply appear to be shouting.

I have not found a copy of the text of this corrido and so do not know the precise meaning of this picture. The only contemporary text I have found printed on the same sheet as the illustration refers to a different incident altogether—one in which police rescued a six-year-old girl who had been tied to a cross somewhere in Mexico City. However, Posada is famous for re-using his illustrations, and there might indeed be a corrido about Teresita for which this scene seemed a suitable decoration. Vanderwood describes the illustration as depicting "the martyred Santa de Cabora." That martyrdom was only figurative, however, for Teresita Urrea did not die until January 1906, when she succumbed to tuberculosis in Clifton, Arizona. She had a long way to travel, both literally and figuratively, before that happened.

A CHANGED LIFE

Meanwhile, the Urrea family, which had gathered in Arizona, kept on moving—first to El Paso, then, in 1897, to the mining town of Clifton, Arizona. Here Teresa married in 1900, only to see her husband go berserk and try to shoot her the day after the wedding. There is a possibility that he had been hired by Díaz agents to abduct Teresita to Mexico or bring proof of her death. Badly shaken (not the least of all because her father had bitterly opposed this marriage), Teresa went to San José, California, to recover. While there, she ministered to a three-year-old boy afflicted with spinal meningitis. After five doctors had pronounced Alvin Rosencrans—son of Mrs. C. P. Rosencrans—incurable, Teresita began her treatments. The child improved. All this was reported in a sympathetic but somewhat sensationalistic article in the *San Francisco Examiner* on Friday, July 27, 1900.

Teresita had been "news" for several years, since before her arrival in Arizona. She continued to produce good copy, as she accepted a sum of money (possibly $10,000) from a small-time San Francisco businessman to take a national faith-healing tour. It is unclear to what extent she was aware that her sponsors were charging people for her services. She traveled to New York, accompanied by a young man from the Clifton area who started as her interpreter and became her lover as well. Her progress was documented by such headlines as "'Santa Teresa,' The Fanatical Mexican 'Miracle Worker,' in New York." Where before she attributed her abilities to a gift from God, she was now vague as to the source of her powers, saying that she was planning to travel to Paris, Egypt, and India to find out. Teresa had, at least for the time being, changed.

In 1902, Don Tomás died of typhoid fever. Teresa, seeming very tired, settled for a while in Los Angeles, and then in 1904 she moved back to Clifton. She had two daughters by her lover, but, though she had obtained a divorce from her demented husband, she never remarried. She was diagnosed with tuberculosis, and she stayed in her new house on Clifton's south side, getting steadily weaker. She died at home on January 11, 1906. She was thirty-three years old. More than four hundred people attended her funeral. There was a feeling, however, expressed in a newspaper article almost a year after her death, that her powers had diminished if not disappeared. Her grave was moved at least once soon after her death and burial, and apparently never became a focus for pilgrimage and petition, as did that of Juan Soldado.

TERESA AFTER DEATH—
A WOMAN OF MANY ROLES

Is this the end of her story? By no means. Teresita Urrea has been the subject of a steady stream of books and articles in both English and Spanish, both during her lifetime and after her death. At least one corrido exists about her and the carnage at Tomochic. At least one tributary poem appeared in the Clifton newspaper shortly after her death. And a wide range of memories of Teresita lives on in Sonora, Arizona, and Chihuahua.

Teresa is remembered by Mexican historians in connection with the revolt at Tomochic, which has officially entered national mythology as an important precursor of the Revolution of 1910. Less emphasis has been placed on Teresita in her role of healer—this borders on "religious fanaticism," until recently an uncomfortable topic in post-revolutionary Mexico. In one government-published comic book, the Church was excoriated, while Teresita was labeled a "mystic," and her followers, "pagans." A 1975 movie, *La Longitud de Guerra,* dealt with Tomochic and Teresita. And in the late 1990s, a store in Tomochic (owned and operated by Sonorans) was called La Farmacia y Papelería Santa Teresita de Cabora.

A feminist slant on Teresita appeared in the 1970s film *Nobody's Girls: Women of the American Frontier*. Here Teresa and four other women are selected for their parts in the pageant of the Western frontier, even though, if Teresa were involved with any frontier, it would be Mexico's northern one! Just as happened in her lifetime, her name has been associated posthumously with causes, ideas, and ideals that she may not have espoused.

Chicana feminists have also adopted Teresita as one of their own. Like that other powerful Chicana symbol, the Virgin of Guadalupe, she was a nurturing figure as well as an ardent supporter of the poor and oppressed. She was of mixed race and spent her last years in Aztlán, the deeply significant region of the American Southwest which, according to contemporary Chicano thought, was also the original homeland of the Aztecs. She had great powers, which she used without thought of recompense for all who asked for help. Little wonder that her story has significance for Chicanas and that she is hailed as a sort of proto-Chicana.

One recent cause in which her persona has been enlisted is civic boosterism. Clifton and its neighboring town, Morenci, are still mining towns, owing most of their economy to the giant Phelps Dodge Company. In the 1980s, a bitter strike against Phelps Dodge split the community, including many families, in two parts. The union lost, and Phelps Dodge earned the dubious distinction of having broken the back of organized labor in Arizona twice in the twentieth century. (The first instance was the famous—or notorious—Bisbee Deportation of 1917.) Very shortly after the strike ended, a massive flood devastated the town. As Clifton struggled to heal itself from these disasters, it became obvious that it needed to look for sources of income beyond the mines. Tourism provided one such source.

Clifton shares with many Western mining towns a picturesque location in the bottom of a valley. It has some interesting old buildings, and many Cliftonians would like to attract more visitors. In 1993, a photograph in the collections of the museum in nearby (as such things go in the West) Silver City, New Mexico, appeared in the Clifton newspaper with a request for identification of the subject. It showed an attractive young woman clad in late-nineteenth-century costume. A member of the Clifton Historical Society, Charles Spezia, identified the subject as Teresita, although she does not greatly resemble other photographs of "la santa." This brought Teresita back into the public eye, and more specifically, into the thoughts of those civic leaders who were looking for a symbol to unite the strike-torn community and at the same time attract visitors to the region.

Town leaders decided to mark Teresa's grave in some way. Unfortunately, its whereabouts were unknown, as it had been moved at least twice due to copper-mine expansion. Luis Pérez, a former journalism professor also deeply interested in Teresita, searched in vain for the site by following clues in old photos and paintings. Finally, a sweet smell in the cemetery led him to what he firmly believes is the site. A slab was poured, a marker erected, and an iron fence placed around the plot. An annual "Fiesta de La Santa de Cabora" began in April 1994. It met with great success. Three years later, the president of the Clifton Chamber of Commerce told a reporter for the *Arizona Republic,* "When you have trials and tribulations, and when there is so much tumult, the peace of Teresita is beyond description." In a sense, her healing mission was thus continuing more than ninety years after her death.

Has it continued in other senses as well? In Clifton's Teresa revival movement, we have mostly heard the voice of the town's professional class—management, if you will. How about el pueblo—the poor and downtrodden who were her most numerous followers during most of her life? It's hard, after the deep divisions and distrust caused by the strike, to interview working folks in Clifton, especially on a subject that might be considered superstitious by outsiders, but we find some indications that her memory remained potent for many years after her death.

One former resident of the area, a Mexican American man in his sixties, recalls his father taking him in the 1950s to a roadside overlook, telling him that there had originally been a small cave or "natural nicho" on the site. People would go there to burn candles and leave offerings to Teresita. He also remembers his father frequently saying, *"Dios en el cielo y Teresita aquí en la tierra"* ("God in heaven and Teresita here on earth"). Another former Cliftonian spoke of a *cuevita de Teresita* where a local curandera once took one of her brothers for healing. The cuevita (or small cave) is now closed off with a fence. The last time she drove past it on the road, she noticed a wreath hanging on the fence. She also told me that, according to what she had been told, the Devil was in the valley, and Teresita

Painting by Cottonwood, Arizona, artist Stoney Harby, of Teresita curing the Rosencrans boy in California. Clifton resident Charles Spezia used this image for a run of postcards.

put a cross on the mountain at each end to drive him away and keep him out. I have heard that those crosses are still maintained in their places.

Sometime in the mid-1990s, an Arizona artist was inspired to paint a picture of Teresita healing the little Rosencrans boy in San José, California. Charles Spezia, the man who identified the "mystery photograph" for the Silver City museum, obtained permission to have the picture printed as a postcard. According to him, the card sold out very rapidly. There is no way of telling how many, if any, of these pictures ended up on home altars. Also probably on home altars somewhere sit the small quantities of dirt from Teresita's grave that the local Catholic church occasionally gets requests for, which it always fills. And Paul Vanderwood reports seeing a scroll of paper— probably a note—tied with ribbon to the fence surrounding her grave.

However, I have heard no evidence that she was called upon for assistance during Clifton's most traumatic recent experience—the strike of the 1980s. Families were split apart by this event, which the Phelps Dodge Company finally won. Barbara Kingsolver, who visited Clifton during much of the strike and who wrote on the role of women in the conflict, reports that she encountered no references to Santa Teresita as a figure to be prayed to in times of stress. She does recall that Teresita would occasionally come up in conversation, but only as a famous person who was buried in a local cemetery.

Teresita has at least one chapel dedicated to her. It stands on a property called the Santa Teresita Ranch, near Cascabel, in southern Arizona's San Pedro Valley. Here is its story, as told to me by a former owner. Sometime before 1994, the property had been owned by a man who discovered that he was suffering from valley fever, a debilitating spore-borne disease endemic to southern Arizona. He promised to build a chapel to some saint—which one I have not discovered—if he were to recover. He did recover, and the chapel was built.

When my informants wanted to buy the property in 1994, the tiny chapel, by then empty and in bad repair, was the only permanent building standing. The would-be purchasers, an Anglo couple, had read about Santa Teresita in a recent issue of *Arizona Highways* magazine. They had been having difficulties in securing a loan to buy the land and prayed to Teresa, promising that if they in fact purchased the land they would rededicate the chapel to her. At that point, "everything turned around," and a bank offered a suitable loan. They purchased the property, which they named

> November 2, El Día de los Muertos, is Mexico's Day of the Dead. Many people believe that on this day, the dead return to visit this world. In some regions, elaborate altars and even feasts are set out for them, in homes or at their graves. In northern Mexico, it is a time for remembering the dead and for cleaning their burial sites. The Catholic All Souls' Day, an equivalent holy day, also occurs on November 2.

in Teresita's honor, and restored the chapel, placing her picture on the altar. Now they no longer own the property, but the current owner, who has family connections with Clifton, maintains the chapel. One of the former owners conducts healings and told me that when she is working, she feels Teresita there with her, offering assistance and advice.

This is not the only instance of Teresita continuing her work of healing in the present. Materias, the mediums of the Fidencista movement, which comes up at length later in this book, are said to channel Teresita, among other spirits. One writer of my acquaintance, a distant collateral descendant of Teresita's, told me that he had been in contact with her spirit in connection with a book project.

And what of Teresita in Sonora, where her fame began? On November 2, 2001, El Día de los Muertos in Mexico, I drove the thirty miles from Fundición, Sonora, on a dirt road to Cabora, the site of the hacienda where Teresita did her healing in the early 1880s. The hacienda itself was gone, reduced to foundations and some building stones that had been recycled into houses and walls in the present-day village of some sixty people. The *casa grande* could still be traced on the ground, however, and it had indeed been huge. Small stretches of tiled flooring were still visible within the foundation lines. The local store was marked "CABORA, SONORA," and people knew that a woman named Teresa Urrea, whom they identified as "Santa Teresita," had once lived there. One or two of the young men who were drinking beer that Saturday afternoon were wearing Jesús Malverde amulets (see Chapter 4 for more on Malverde). There was no sign of a shrine or altar or offerings in Teresita's memory.

One kilometer south and west of the village was a small ranch headquarters called "El Campo de Santa Teresita." This was owned by members of Teresita's family, but lived in and administered by others. In the neat house was a painting done from a photograph of Teresita. The family is said to own the original photo. In the silver-mining town of Alamos, several miles away, descendants of the Urreas still live. The local museum has a

Interior of the Teresita chapel in Cascabel, Arizona. The image to the left shows the Virgin of San Juan de los Lagos, and the *Arizona Highways* article hangs at the right. (October 2002)

photograph of Teresita on display, together with an interpretive text explaining who she was. In southern Sonora mestizo culture, she has become a historical figure, with no spiritual significance that I have been able to find.

So there we have Teresita Urrea, La Santa de Cabora. She was famous in her lifetime and influential in the course of Mexican history, and she was used by many people with many different agendas. Since her death, her memory has served even more purposes. Living or dead, she seems to have been reinterpreted and manipulated by almost everyone with whom she came into contact. Nevertheless, she still has a presence in the region where she once lived.

Jesús Malverde, from a devotional card purchased at his chapel in Culiacán in 1995.

CHAPTER 4

JESÚS MALVERDE
El Bandido Generoso

Voy a cantarles la historia	I'll sing you the story
De un hombre muy conocido	Of a very well-known man
De nombre Jesús Malverde	Jesús Malverde by name
Un generoso bandido.	A generous bandit.
El nunca conoció el miedo	He never knew fear
Pues dondequiera robaba	Since he robbed just anywhere
Asaltaba diligencias	He attacked stagecoaches
Y a los pobres ayudaba.	And he helped the poor.

So go the first verses of *"La Entrega de Malverde"* ("The Betrayal of Malverde") by Arturo Franco—only one of several songs that folk composers have written about Malverde. Many of these songs have been commercially recorded. Malverde is indeed famous. His shrine is included in an English-language guidebook to the state of Sinaloa published by the state. Journalists have published articles about him in a score of newspapers—even in *Esquire* magazine. And, unlike the other five "saints" this book deals with, historians cannot reach any consensus that the man ever existed. That issue is supremely unimportant to his present-day devotees, however, and especially to those responsible for all the journalistic attention paid him in recent years. For whether or not he ever existed in history, Jesús Malverde lives today as, among other things, the patron and protector of los narcotraficantes—the people engaged in the international drug trade.

Those who affirm his reality say that he was a bandit active in the area around Culiacán, Sinaloa, in the early years of the twentieth century—Jesús Juárez Maso, born on December 24, 1870. Some versions of his life say that he was born in Jalisco and brought to Sinaloa as a child; others, that he was a native of the area around Mocorito, Sinaloa, a town to the north of Culiacán. He was given the nickname of *Malverde*—"Bad Green One"—because he hid in the brush—the "green"—in order to accomplish his robberies. A more fanciful version has it that he would disguise himself by tying banana leaves all over his body. Author Fabrizio Mejía Madrid repeats this version and goes on to say that it wasn't until the 1920s that Juárez the bandit entered legend as "Malverde." Another Mexican author suggests that the color green itself is traditionally associated with evil. However the name came to be—and *apodos* or nicknames are extremely common in Mexico, often better-known than an individual's Christian or family names—it stuck. Jesús Malverde he became, and Jesús Malverde he remains.

His devotees will tell you that Malverde was a generous bandit: he robbed from the rich and gave to the poor. Some skeptics believe that Malverde as he is understood today is an artifact—a combination of the exploits and stories of two other Sinaloans. One, celebrated in song and story, was Heraclio Bernal, who flourished in late-nineteenth-century Sinaloa until his capture and execution in 1888. He waged war on wealthy *hacendados* (landowners), and, in 1885, signed a document proclaiming the power of Don Porfirio and the authorities of Sinaloa to be illegitimate. Some of the details of his career find echoes in the Malverde legends.

The other was Felipe Bachomo, a Mayo Indian revolutionary leader in the period 1913–1915. Bachomo's theater of operations was in northern Sinaloa, near the Río Fuerte. While neither of these men were strictly bandits, they did support their causes by robbing the wealthy and were viewed by the authorities as mere lawbreakers. Each is said to have been betrayed by one of his followers. That is one explanation of Malverde. Another is that that Malverde did exist…but only as an invention of Sinaloa's governor Francisco Cañedo, created by him to keep wealthy hacienda owners in line.

The Malverde legend, however, persists in opposing him to the governor. On one occasion, it is said, when Cañedo had a price on Malverde's head, the bandit broke into the Governor's Mansion, stole his sword, and wrote on the wall "Jesús M. was here." Neither the guards nor the dogs in the mansion noticed his presence. Another version tells us that Malverde worked as a mason and therefore knew his way around all the buildings in town. When the governor offered to pardon the bandit if he dared to rob the governor's mansion, Malverde easily crept in, stole the sword, and left his message. Or the governor offered a pardon in exchange for not robbing the mansion, and Malverde showed his contempt by breaking in and stealing the governor's daughter. Although she was returned unharmed, the governor swore bitter enmity against him. Shades of Robin Hood and Zorro! And it was the governor's forces, many say, that finally caused Malverde's death on May 3, 1909.

But once again, accounts differ. Some say he was betrayed by his *compadre*, Baldemar López. Others say that his henchman cut off his feet and dragged him to town in order to collect a 10,000-peso reward. Yet another version has it that when Malverde was dying of a gangrenous wound in his leg, he instructed his partner to kill him, cut off his head, collect the reward offered by the governor, and distribute the money to the poor. After death, his body was hung from a mesquite tree and left there as a warning on Governor Cañedo's orders. People were afraid to cut him down and bury him, for fear they, too, would be shot by the dreaded *rurales*—Don Porfirio's bloodily efficient rural police. Cañedo himself died a little more than a month after Malverde. His funeral is said to have been attended by the major chiefs of Sinaloa's Chinese opium gangs.

Malverde dead was not, however, Malverde forgotten. Accounts differ as to precisely what his first miracle was. One writer states that he helped a farmer—or an old woman—find a lost cow. A more common story, repeatedly told by Eligio González, the man who took care of Malverde's shrine in Culiacán in the 1990s, is this: A friend of Malverde's was driving some mules loaded with gold and silver to the coast from Canelas, in the inland state of Durango. The mules had gone astray one night, and their owner was understandably eager to find them again. At that time, Malverde's bones were still hanging from the mesquite tree, and the governor had issued orders that nobody cut them down. So the man asked Malverde to help him. Next morning, the mules and their cargo were found safe and sound. The grateful *arriero* (muleteer) cut Malverde's bones down and quietly buried them in the same cemetery where the governor is buried. To this day, according to the story, nobody knows for certain the whereabouts of Malverde's remains.

As one might expect, we also hear other stories of Malverde's burial. One is that he was buried under the mesquite tree. One writer suggests that because Malverde's remains were not permitted to be buried, people placed rocks on his body until it was covered. One can also relate the pile of rocks—or pebbles—at Malverde's death site to the northwestern Mexican custom of erecting a cross and often a rock pile as well on the site where some person met a sudden death. Passers-by traditionally say a prayer for the repose of the soul of the dead person and add a rock to the pile. However the rocks got there, there is supposed to have been a pile of rocks surmounted by a metal cross at Malverde's death site long before a chapel was built.

The site looked like that in 1956, when Sinaloan journalist Ernesto Álvarez Nolasco wrote an article on Malverde in a regional journal. He described a metal cross on a pile of rocks, with several smaller crosses placed around it, and offerings of candles, silver milagros, flowers, and wreaths. He also described an evolution of the death site shrine from a simple pile of rocks, each rock representing a prayer for Malverde's soul on the part of a passerby, to a place of petitions. In his account, the first person to be posthumously helped by the *bandido generoso* (generous bandit) was an older woman named Tomasa. Malverde appeared to her and told her where a clay pot filled with gold coins was buried. In exchange all he asked of her was a visit to his death site. Word of this miracle spread rapidly, said Álvarez, and the site rapidly became a place of petitions. The author of the article did not mention the underworld as participating in the devotion to Malverde—just the poor.

The death site itself was out in the *monte*—the wilderness, far from Culiacán's city limits. It was of little importance—just a little cross where passersby would leave little stones. According to one man who remembered it from his childhood, the first people to pray there were mostly *muchachas de la vida galante,* or prostitutes. As Culiacán's population grew after the middle of the twentieth century, the site came to be within the limits of the expanding city. Then the state government decided to build a new state office building on the land that had been used for Malverde's shrine. Strong protests to the plan lasted for two years, with the local media taking sides. I have been told that, after the building was finished, the glass in the windows on the side where Malverde's shrine had been kept breaking. Finally, the state provided land for Malverde where the shrine now stands, as well as land for the rock pile. The moving of the rock pile was in itself pretty exciting. All of Culiacán gathered to watch. One account reports that the stones jumped "like popcorn" when the bulldozer tried to shift them. The bulldozer operator had to get drunk to get his courage up before attacking the stones, according to accounts of the incident, and the bulldozer itself broke down as soon as it touched the grave.

The present shrine to Malverde was built in 1980 at least partly with state money. It replaced a much smaller chapel on the same site. In recent years, a number of journalists and other authors have visited the Malverde

Capilla and published on it. They pay great attention to the story of the late Eligio González, builder and self-appointed guardian of the chapel, and the source of much Malverde lore. González credited Malverde with having saved his life when, driving a passenger truck in the sierra, he was attacked by robbers and shot four times. He credited his survival to Malverde and dedicated the rest of his life to serving his cause. He built the chapel in the 1980s and used the money offerings left there for the support of the poor in the form of free burials and the distribution of food, toys, and other goods. He died in 2002.

One interesting detail mentioned by one source is the presence of a number of small rocks in the chapel. Malverde was a thief, he was told, and therefore one gets his attention by "stealing" a rock from his *capilla*. If one gets the desired miracle, one returns that rock and brings another. The northwest Mexican tradition of rock pile memorials persists with a new twist, appropriate to the occasion.

La Capilla de Malverde

I first encountered Jesús Malverde in the very early 1990s, when I found a prayer card with his picture on it. Shortly thereafter I saw a photograph of a shrine to him in Chihuahua. However, not until March 2003, after much reading and many discussions concerning this generous bandit, was I able to go to Culiacán and visit the Malverde chapel there. At the time of my visit, the building was perhaps thirty feet long and fifteen to twenty feet high. The façade consisted of many small panes of glass and had three doors. Two booths selling souvenirs stood in front of the chapel, and several feet of the lower part of the façade were taken up with ex-votos. These were almost invariably generic in nature, thanking Malverde (or God and Malverde) for unspecified favors received. More often than not, they were signed, not by an individual but by a family.

Once through the doors of the chapel, one was confronted with a smaller chapel, painted white with a doorway and pitched roof trimmed in green. An accordion and a *bajo sexto* (the bass, twelve-stringed guitar used in *norteño* music) hung just outside the door. Within, three busts of Malverde sat on a black-tiled altar, along with a statue of the Santo Niño de Atocha, other religious figures, and a pile of river-rounded stones. A life-sized statue of the Virgin of Guadalupe stood to one side. The black-tiled walls were occupied by more ex-votos—these ones made of photoengraved metal. Like the ones outside the chapel, they thanked Malverde for unspecified favors and were often signed by families. Some mentioned or bore images of other supernaturals, including the Virgin of Guadalupe and La Santísima Muerte. Other figures thanked elsewhere in the chapel include San Judas Tadeo (Saint Jude) and the Sacred Heart of Jesus. Many of these metal ex-votos include a phrase like *"de Sinaloa a California,"* or *"de Culiacán a Modesto."* These can indicate emigration routes, or they can suggest the routes that successful shipments have traveled. Reinforcing the latter idea is the recurrent phrase of thanks for "lighting my road" and the presence of at least one image of a truck on an ex-voto.

But we can find good evidence that people other than drug traders call on Malverde for help. A jar on a top shelf in the outer chapel contains a gigantic pickled shrimp—a shrimp also mentioned in earlier articles about the shrine. A lovely small painting of a shrimp or fishing boat named *Tapachula*

> ⚏ **Saint Jude** *(San Judas Tadeo)* was one of the twelve apostles. He is usually shown dressed in green and white robes, holding a staff, and pointing to a large religious medal on his chest. A "flame of enlightenment" springs from his forehead. Respected as patron of impossible causes, he appears all over the Mexican world. In the borderlands, he is second in popularity only to the Virgin of Guadalupe.
>
> ⚏ **The Sacred Heart of Jesus** *(El Sagrado Corazón de Jesús)* is a Catholic devotion that emphasizes Christ's love for humanity. In Sacred Heart representations, an image of Jesus looks directly at the viewer, while pointing to his exposed heart, which burns with love.

contains a message of thanks to Malverde for having always lent a hand when it was needed. But the huge majority of ex-votos are carefully nonspecific as to the nature of the help given.

The inner chapel stands in the middle of the larger building. The alcoves to either side are for the most part filled with more ex-votos—some simply attached to the walls and some in built-in, glass-fronted niches. These latter obviously represent a larger investment in the shrine. One six-by-three-foot cardboard panel contains color photos of various situations and occasions on which people have been helped by distributions of money, food, toys, or other goods from the shrine.

For the Malverde chapel is continuing Malverde's tradition of helping the poorest of the poor. Caretaker Eligio González supported himself by selling newspapers, then redistributed all the funds he collected at the chapel. His son, Jesús Manuel González Sánchez, is said to do the same, and he has erected a sign detailing the chapel's charitable activities. Another indication of these activities is a brass bell that hangs beside a large cross bearing Malverde's name and dates,

Teresita Sánchez, keeper of the store at the Malverde chapel in Culiacán, presents a gift of money to Malverde. Dollar bills cover the wall behind the altar. (March 2003)

to the right of the inner chapel. This bell is rung when a pauper is brought to the chapel for burial—another of the chapel's functions.

Beyond the cross sits a store selling Malverde pictures, belt buckles, scapulars, necklaces, ball caps, T-shirts, cassettes and CDs, and other mementos. Many of the items combine the images of Malverde and the Virgin of Guadalupe. I purchased a T-shirt, for example, featuring a large *Guadalupana* with the bust of Malverde in front of her. Beside the store, a small altar bears a bust of Malverde, a statue of Saint Jude, holy water, a rosary, and pictures of San Martín Caballero and San Ciprian. The wall behind the altar is lined with one- and five-dollar bills. If one wishes one's souvenirs blessed, Teresita Sánchez Valles will do so at the altar. When I purchased a Malverde ball cap, she placed it on the statue's head during the blessing process. The same bust has a slot at the top, in which she deposits any donations given to the work of the chapel.

While I was in the chapel, a man asked me to photograph him in front of the altar. He handed me his flash camera and I did so. When I asked to take his portrait with my own camera, he smiled and said, "Next time." Another man, younger and soberly dressed and wearing dark glasses, purchased some 5,000 pesos worth of objects from the store—worth $500 at the current rate of exchange. My companions speculated that he was in the drug trade.

EL NARCOSANTÓN?

Most treatments of Malverde in the media, especially in the United States, emphasize his following among the ranks of the narcotraficantes. This connection is perfectly true, though not the total story. He is in fact patron of the *narcos*. Elijah Wald, in his informative book *Narcocorrido,* explains the move from "friend of the poor" to *narcosanto* in this way: "If ever there was a class of poor people who needed a supernatural guardian, it was the drug traffickers, and Malverde had a natural affinity for those on the dark side

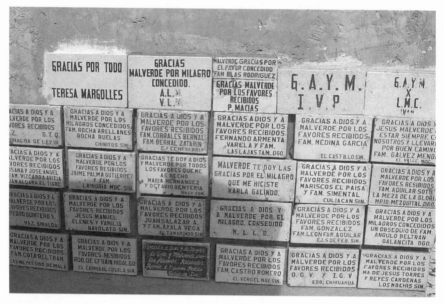

Ex-voto plaques on the front wall of the Malverde chapel in Culiacán. (March 2003)

of the law." His identification with the drug world is strong enough that a law enforcement officer in Arizona once discussed with me the notion that finding a picture of Malverde in a man's wallet, along with the phone number of a known drug house, might be sufficient grounds for indictment.

But Malverde's patronage extends to other worlds as well. I have been told that the "tunnel kids" of Nogales, Sonora, consider him their patron. These children live in the storm drains of that border city and make a living through drugs, prostitution, and whatever means are open to them. They refer to themselves as *el barrio libre*—"the free neighborhood"—and many carry the image of "El Santo Malverde."

Others among his devotees do not seem outside the law in any sense, but rather outside any normal network of assistance—in other words, Mexico's working classes. For example, in the 1980s, a young oyster diver working out of Mazatlán, Sinaloa, got tangled up in his rope and was in danger of drowning. He saw the face of Malverde in a vision, freed himself, and for at least eleven years helped take care of the Culiacán chapel. Another man, sixty-four years old, attributed the birth of his eighth child (by a much younger wife) to Malverde's assistance and brought the thirteen-day-old baby to the shrine to give thanks. Objects left as thank offerings at the shrine include ears of corn, presumably from farmers, and the huge pickled shrimp mentioned earlier.

On the other hand, the words "DE SINALOA A CALIFORNIA," which appear on so many ex-voto plaques, may well be coded references to successful drug runs. Perhaps the last word on this subject comes from Sergeant Manny Flores, a Department of Public Safety drug specialist in Phoenix, who agreed that many people outside the drug world look to Malverde for help. However, he added, "When I see someone wearing a Malverde pendant, a white cowboy hat, $400 boots, and gold chains, I suspect they're connected with the drug trade."

And what do Sinaloans think of Malverde? The day of my visit to the chapel, I interviewed four Culiacán intellectuals: a professional historian, an archivist, an actor, and an author. They seemed rather proud of him. "Sinaloans are an irreverent and independent people," the director of the State Historical Archives told me. Malverde serves as an appropriate symbol of Sinaloan identity and also an appropriate supernatural individual for the very poor. Malverde, he said, demands nothing and sets up no moral rules, but simply gives what is needed. He even ventured to link Malverde's name with possible prehistoric nature deities, for example the god of the pitahaya cactus.

The historian reminded me that the Malverde of legend was a "bandido generoso" who served the poor. Malverde today, in his spirit, helps the very same segment of Mexican society—those at the bottom of the social and economic heap.

The actor reaffirmed the appeal of Malverde as a supernatural being, saying that he made no demands and asked for no confession. He simply was as he had been—a generous bandit. The actor went on to suggest an idea I find fascinating—that by creating a situation in which wealthy drug dealers give large sums of money to the chapel to be redistributed among the poor, Malverde is doing precisely what he did in his life.

Finally, the novelist told me that he remembers Malverde's grave and attendant rock pile as existing in a very rough barrio in the 1950s—a barrio into which he and his friends did not dare to go. Malverde, he feels, achieved the true mythic status he has today when the government tried to move the site in order to erect an official building there. Resistance to government insensitivity is always popular, and through his ghostly resistance, Malverde achieved the popularity he has today.

All four of these men agreed that, whether or not Malverde had actually existed as a bandit at the turn of the century, he exists today as an individual to be reckoned with. Another common theme in the discussions was the comparison of Malverde with other Mexican Robin Hood types from the Porfiriato—such as Chucho el Roto in Mexico City, Heraclio Bernal in Sinaloa, and Pancho Villa in Chihuahua. A final common theme was the contrast between a Catholic Church that imposes moral standards on people, and Malverde, the spirit who simply gives.

PRAYER CARDS & AMULETS

Jesús Malverde is depicted as a man in his thirties, perhaps, with black hair, dark eyes, and a thin black moustache. He wears a kerchief, usually black, around his neck, with the ends hanging down in front of his shirt like a necktie. His shirt appears to be "Western style," with pocket flaps. I've seen two standard Malverde representations: one a full-length drawing and the other a bust. In the full-length portrayals, the bandit stands with his hands behind his back and a noose around his neck. The other end of the rope has been thrown over a tree branch above his head. A bunch of cattails may be seen on his left; the trunk of his hanging tree is to his right. This image usually appears on prayer cards, where-as amulets and some cards display photographs of the bust of Malverde. These busts display a similar image, but with no noose in evidence, and the kerchief and pocket flaps are usually black.

DI TU VOLUNTAD

Ayudar a mi gente en el nombre de DIOS

JESUS MALVERDE

The most common prayer card of Malverde, showing him about to be hung.

Elijah Wald relates a story that appears to go far toward explaining how this image—an image, mind you, of a man who may never have existed—became fixed in the public mind. After the present chapel was built, people started flocking to it. As is usual with Mexican pilgrims, many wanted something—some image of Malverde—to take home with them, perhaps to put on their altars. But no such image existed. So one Carlos García asked around for a photograph of Malverde, so he could have busts made in the great commercial crafts center of Guadalajara. Not finding any photos (although there was a rumor that one such existed), he asked a craftsman to make him a bust. García felt that Malverde had been young, good-looking, and with light skin. As the great *ranchera* singers Jorge Negrete and Pedro Infante were extremely popular at the time, he requested that the bust resemble both these men. He was pleased with the result and made his first order of two hundred busts.

These sold in a week. So he ordered five hundred more, and then a thousand. Then Eligio González, guardian of the capilla, started ordering his own busts. Today, Malverde busts are a big business and available in many cities in the United States, as well as all over northwestern Mexico. I have seen what appear to be the results of several different molds, but all with the same characteristics: black hair and moustache, light skin, black neckerchief and pocket flaps. I do not know whether or not the hanging picture was derived from the busts; it seems possible.

Of course, we also find another version of this story. Caretaker Eligio González told one writer that he himself had ordered the busts made, using as a model an old photograph he had acquired from the woman who had told him about Malverde in the first place—Doña Amadita. She showed him the picture, and later on he ordered the images made according to what he remembered seeing.

The images of Malverde appear on a multitude of objects. The two most common are color photographs of the bust and prayer cards that show the full-length drawing. The cards with the drawing have the words *DI TU VOLUNDAD ayudar a mi gente en el nombre de DIOS*—"SAY YOUR DESIRE help my people in the name of GOD."

The following prayer is often printed on the card:

LA VERDADERA ORACIÓN	THE TRUE PRAYER
DEL ÁNIMA DE MALVERDE	OF THE SPIRIT OF MALVERDE
Hoy ante tu Cruz prostrado	Today, lying before your Cross
Oh! Malverde mi Señor	Oh! Malverde my Lord
Te pido misericordia	I ask mercy of you
Y que alivies mi dolor.	And that you lighten my sorrow.
Tú que moras en la Gloria	You who dwell in Heaven
Y estás muy cerca de Dios	And are very close to God
Escucha los sufrimientos	Hear the sufferings
De este humilde pecador.	Of this humble sinner.

Oh! Malverde milagroso	Oh! Miraculous Malverde
Oh! Malverde mi Señor	Oh! Malverde my Lord
Cencédeme este favor	Grant me this favor
Y llena mi alma de gozo.	And fill my soul with joy.
Dame salud Señor,	Give me health, Lord,
Dame reposo	Give me rest
Dame bienestar	Give me well-being
Y seré dichoso.	And I will be happy.

In very specific language, this prayer (which has the form of an *alabanza* or hymn of praise) describes Malverde as being in Heaven and in the presence of God. In other words, as far as his devotees are concerned, Jesús Malverde is a saint. The whole issue of sainthood will be discussed later in this chapter. For now, suffice it to say that there is very little chance of Malverde's ever being elevated to sainthood by the official Catholic Church. This is, of course, of no importance whatever to his devotees, especially to those who believe themselves to have been the beneficiaries of Malverde's miracles.

Photographs of Malverde's bust, often as it appears on the altar in his chapel in Culiacán, adorn a wide variety of cards, scapulars, and amulets. These latter are often framed in braided leather or plastic and hung from loops of the same materials. I have seen large numbers of these highly popular items at market stands in several Sonoran cities, and even being hawked on street corners by young boys. Vendors and others have told me that at least some of the braiding is the work of prisoners trying to earn a little pocket money. While some of the amulets only contain a picture of Malverde, others have an image of San Judas or the Virgen de Guadalupe on the other side.

In swap meets in large U.S. cities, one finds other Malverde memorabilia: gold pendants, caps, even silk shirts bearing Malverde's familiar face. One vendor's stall had a sign saying MALVERDE ES AMOR, or "Malverde is love." A silk shirt in my possession, purchased at a Phoenix swap meet, has Malverde's face, wreathed in stylized marijuana leaves, on the front, back, and sleeves.

We also find one other important kind of Malverde memorabilia—recorded musical tributes. Visitors to the chapel since the early 1990s have mentioned the availability of cassettes bearing songs dedicated to Malverde. Many of these songs are corridos—the story songs of Mexican folk expression. Although corridos have celebrated the deeds of bandits and other rebels against society since the nineteenth century, the form has undergone a recent reflorescence with the popularity of the narcocorrido. The tributes to Malverde fit neatly into this category, of course.

At the time of my visit to Malverde's chapel, only one recording was available…in both CD and cassette form. The cassette bore no information concerning either songs or artists; the CD carried an artist list, but no song titles. The artists listed included such well-known contemporary groups as Los Incomparables de Tijuana and Miguel and Miguel, but they also included Los Serranitos de Malverde and Los Jilgueritos de Malverde (Malverde's Little Highlanders and Malverde's Little Songbirds). The twenty-six songs include devotional pieces addressed to Malverde as well as corridos describing his life. Many well-known groups who sing narcocorridos will include an occasional Malverde piece in their recorded repertoires; such pieces may well make up the sources of this home-produced CD.

MALVERDE CAPILLAS ALONG THE BORDER

I've heard of several smaller shrines and chapels dedicated to Malverde in addition to the Culiacán chapel—some of them reportedly in ranches owned by drug lords or in barrios where drug trafficking is a common occupation. Altars to him may be found in drug-related houses and apartments on both sides of the border. Others are more accessible to the ordinary traveler. One such chapel stands on the southbound lane of Highway 15 as it passes through Fundición, Sonora, between Ciudad Obregón and Navojoa. This small white building has a cross at the gable and JESÚS MALVERDE written over the door. Inside, a black cross and a bust of Malverde stand on the altar, along with a few floral offerings. The bust is protected by metal bars. A picture of Malverde's hanging scene, done in colored thread, hangs to the left of the altar; the prayer quoted earlier hangs in a frame to the right. Malverde's portrait is roughly sketched in pencil on the north wall. Other graffiti thank Malverde for having provided the writer's family with sustenance.

According to a local resident, the chapel was built in the early 1990s as the result of a *manda* (or vow) made by a woman from Sinaloa. She provided the materials and some local men did the actual construction. The nature of the manda was not discussed.

Another smaller chapel and a separate nicho, also built in fulfillment of a manda, stand on a hill near the Magdalena–Tubutama highway as it passes through Barrio San Ysidro, just west of Magdalena, Sonora. On my earlier visits, one or the other of these had a Malverde bust on its altar. Beside the chapel stands a six-foot-high white wooden cross; between the two buildings are some flat, tiled steps bearing pencil sketches of Malverde. I was told that the young man responsible for this chapel was involved in the drug trade. In May 2003, both chapels had been stripped bare.

Malverde appears again on the altar in the kitchen of a roadside restaurant at a major highway junction in Sonora, as well as in the capilla attached to that restaurant. The restaurant serves long-distance truck drivers and is decorated with photographs of different rigs. In this case, Malverde shares space on the altar with San Judas and the Virgen de Guadalupe and in the capilla with San Judas. At the time of my visit, his bust was placed out of sight near the door of the chapel, but the one on the kitchen altar was visible to all.

A final roadside Malverde shrine stands on Highway 2, several miles east of Agua Prieta, Sonora. This is the northernmost of the roads connecting

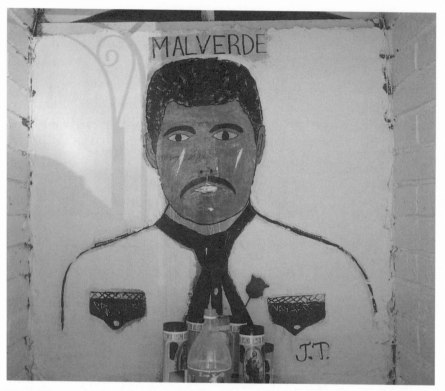

Back wall of a roadside shrine on Mexico's Highway 2, just east of Agua Prieta, Sonora. (January 2002)

Sonora with Chihuahua, and as such a major commercial thoroughfare. This nicho is of red brick and stands about three feet high. It is empty except for candles; the entire back wall of the whitewashed interior is filled with a mural painting of Malverde. I've sometimes seen devotional graffiti, and on other visits they have been painted out. In March 2002, Alfredo Gonzales and I were about to photograph the nicho and copy down the graffiti when a red Ford Explorer with four young men in the front seat drove up. All were dressed in jeans, boots, and Western shirts, some wearing gold jewelry. All had been drinking. They offered us a beer and asked if we were "visiting the santos." We declined the offer and agreed that such was our motive for stopping. One of the men asked us if we had matches, then placed two candles in front of the nicho and started talking with Malverde, standing with arms outstretched. The translated gist of his first sentence was "Malverde, I haven't visited you for a long time, but I'm here now. I brought you some candles…but I can't light them for you because I don't have any matches." At about this time my companion and I drove off. On our return three days later, the graffiti, which had covered the walls on our previous visit, had all been painted over.

SAINTS IN THE CATHOLIC CHURCH

It should be obvious that figures like Malverde are not likely to be considered among the number of saints by the official Catholic Church. The man, after all, was a bandit and probably a murderer, if indeed he existed at all. Not that such individuals have not become saints of the Church, but a period of repentance and dedication to religion must follow, or the individual's cause must have strong institutional backing of some sort. None of this is evident in Malverde's story.

Nevertheless, it might be useful at this point to pause and examine the role of saints in official Catholic thought—who they are, how they become saints, and why their help is invoked by the faithful. Saints are men and women who lived such exemplary Christian lives that when they died they are believed to have gone straight to heaven—into the presence of God. Because they were once people like us, subject to all the miseries and frustrations that are part of the human condition, they are believed to be especially sympathetic to our needs. Because they are in the presence of God, they can intercede with Him in our behalf. Saints do not work miracles; only God can do that. But saints can act as our advocates before the Throne.

The first saint—and the only one who can be called such with total assurance—was Saint Dismas, the good thief who was crucified with Christ, and to whom He promised a place in Paradise. All others are merely assumed to be saints on the basis of their lives on Earth and of the miracles they are believed to have influenced. In the earliest days of the Church, Christian martyrdom (as in the case of the Apostles and many more) was sufficient to have one acclaimed a saint. Great importance would be attached to the place of the martyr's death (and often, burial)—the spot where that person became a saint in heaven. One might think that the fact that three of our folk saints died violent deaths might qualify them as martyrs. It might, in some senses, but not in the eyes of the Church. After all, Malverde was executed for his *crimes,* while Pancho Villa, the subject of the next chapter, was assassinated for political reasons. Only Juan Soldado, if indeed innocent, might qualify as a martyr of sorts. But here the Church has something definite to say. Father Alban Butler, in his account of Saint Maria Goretti, a young Italian girl stabbed to death while resisting rape, makes it clear that "a violent and unjust death alone" is not enough to constitute martyrdom. Maria Goretti was remembered as a very pious young woman who died in defense of chastity, a Christian virtue. She also forgave her murderer as she died.

After the persecution of Christians ended in the Roman Empire, the emphasis shifted from witnessing Christ through martyrdom to doing so in other ways. One could be acclaimed a saint because of an ascetic life or through one's influence as a bishop or missionary. Most saints started with local followers only; their reputations expanded through trade or through the movement of communities of monks or nuns, especially in the case of saints associated with large numbers of miracles. As Christianity spread through and beyond the Mediterranean world, local deities were at times co-opted as saints. Saint Brigid of Ireland, for example, seems to be directly descended from a Celtic goddess with the same name and supernatural responsibilities.

For many centuries, saints were acclaimed locally, first by the Christian community as a whole and later by the bishops. A saint's reputation and devotion either spread or stayed purely local. The first canonization to officially be ratified by the pope was that of Saint Udalricus (Ulric) in A.D. 993. By 1234, papal control of the process of canonization or the creation of saints was complete. Even now, however, the process always begins at the local level or within that person's religious order. If there is deemed sufficient evidence of sanctity,

Ulric, Bishop of Augsburg, was born in A.D. 890. A diligent pastor of his diocese, he ministered to the sick, daily washed the feet of the poor, and devoted his time insofar as it was possible to preaching, visiting, and instructing. He died in 973.

the person is declared "venerable" by the Congregation for the Causes of Saints in Rome. The person's life is then examined for possible beatification, which involves a declaration by the pope that the person is indeed in heaven. Beatification requires, among other things, two proven miracles. A beatified person is called "blessed" and may be venerated by the faithful only at his or her place of birth or in the religious houses he or she founded.

The final step is canonization, which involves long, carefully researched arguments and counterarguments, and which must involve two authenticated miracles. The purpose of the miracles is simple; they are proof that the individual is indeed in heaven and has interceded successfully with God on the petitioner's behalf. With canonization, the pope infallibly declares the person involved to be in heaven, thus ordering his or her veneration by the entire Church.

Obviously, such a process, taking place to a great extent within the Church bureaucracy in Rome, leaves a good deal of room for politics to enter in. The Church is filled with factions, some bitterly hostile to one another. Members of religious orders will, of course, press for their own. Members of powerful factions become offended by other powerful individuals pushing for certain canonizations or beatifications, and do all they can to block these, simply because of who supports them. The pope or the bureaucracy may wish to balance the elevation of a liberal with that of a reactionary, as happened in the 1990s when Pope John Paul II simultaneously beatified John XXIII, the great liberal reformer, and the ultrareactionary Pius IX.

Folk Saints of the Borderlands

Although the modern Church clearly proclaims the universality of holiness, an examination of the Church calendar will show that reality has yet to catch up with the ideal. A majority of saints are European in origin, and celibate white males predominate. Woman saints tend to be virgins, martyrs, or members of religious orders. Most saints belonged to the middle or upper classes. The list of universally significant saints includes relatively few people of color, poor people, or people who have manifested their holiness through married life.

Many saints are known to the Church through tradition alone. These include such popular saints as Saint Barbara and Saint Christopher, for whose existence we have no solid evidence. Following the general reforms of the Second Vatican Council, Pope Paul VI in 1969 removed many saints, including the two mentioned above, from the official Roman Calendar. This does not mean, however, that they are no longer saints, but rather that in many cases the only thing certain about them is the existence in tradition of their names. Although they no longer have places in the calendar, they have not been "demoted" from sainthood.

Saints are, however, only one category of the faithful departed. There are also those who have died in Christ, but who are still undergoing cleansing and purification in Purgatory. These individuals may be helped by the

Saint Barbara, according to legend, was the daughter of a wealthy pagan of the third or fourth century A.D. When she refused to renounce her Christian faith, her father locked her in a tower, then had her tortured and killed. He was destroyed in a lightning flash. For this reason, Barbara has long been the patron of miners, artillerymen, and others who work with explosives.

Saint Christopher is supposed to have been a man of great strength who carried a child across a river. When Christopher's burden became unbearably heavy, the child identified himself as Christ and told Christopher (whose name means "Christ-bearer") that he had carried the weight of the world on his shoulders. Christopher (the patron of travelers) and Barbara both seem to have been the creations of pious medieval legend-makers.

prayers of the living—in other words, they may be prayed for. They may also be prayed *to* in order that they may intercede for the living when they do reach heaven (and possibly they are already there). This set of beliefs seems to constitute the strongest connection between the individuals in this book and official Catholic theology.

> ⊞ **Santiago de Compostela (Saint James the Greater)** is the apostle James the Greater, said to have preached in Spain before his martyrdom in Palestine. His body was then returned to Spain, where it was discovered 800 years later. He is the patron of Spain and of the militant expansion of Spanish Christianity.

Saints are believed to specialize—to be concerned with certain occupations, places, and issues, often ones with which they were associated in life. The pope declares these patronages, although many are ancient and customary. Thus Saint James the Greater (Santiago) is patron of Spain; Saints Lawrence, Martha, and Pascal Baylon are patrons of cooks; and Saint Peregrine is invoked in cases of cancer. As new occupations and dangers come upon the scene, the pope may announce those saints specifically concerned with them. For instance, because Saint Clare saw a Christmas scene on the wall of her cell in Assisi when she was ill and could not visit the official Christmas nativity display, she has been declared the patron of television.

Some patronages are customary rather than official. Saint Anthony is recognized through much of the Catholic world as the individual to pray to if one has trouble finding a lost object. A common prayer in English is "Saint Anthony, Saint Anthony, look around. Something's lost and can't be found."

> ⊞ **A personal follower of Saint Francis of Assisi, Saint Clare** founded the order of the Poor Clares. Pope Pius XII proclaimed her patron of television in 1958.

Such beliefs are subject to local variations. In Sonora, for instance, the saint addressed for help in finding lost objects is San Pafnuncio (Saint Paphnuntius), a fourth-century Egyptian hermit and bishop. Another traditional finder of lost objects in northern Sonora and southern Arizona is San Cayetano, or Saint Cajetan. The custom in his case is to bet him some small devotional act that he can't find the object in question. He can't resist a bet, people believe, and therefore the object invariably appears. And to end up on an even more specifically local level, in Opodepe, Sonora, those wishing to find lost objects address El Arrastradito, as we learned in the chapter on Juan Soldado.

> ⧖ A fourth-century saint, Peregrine was an eloquent preacher and indefatigable in bringing sinners back into the fold. Suffering from a horribly painful cancer of the foot, he was set to undergo amputation but discovered upon awakening from a light slumber that the cancer had completely disappeared. His patronage of cancer sufferers, though not officially recognized by the Church, follows from this incident.

Here, popular belief and custom seem to be moving away from official Church doctrine. Listening to people talk, I often get the impression that Saint Anthony or Saint Cajetan actually find the objects themselves, rather than interceding on behalf of the petitioner. And so once more we seem to be leaving the world of official doctrine and entering the more pragmatic world of day-to-day belief and custom.

> ⧖ Saint Lawrence was a deacon of the Church, martyred in Rome in A.D. 258. He was literally cooked to death on a gridiron—a fate he suffered calmly.
>
> ⧖ Saint Martha, the sister of Lazarus and Mary, offered hospitality, with perhaps too much compulsive attention to housekeeping details, to Jesus, who gently chided her for this.
>
> ⧖ Saint Pascal Baylon (San Pascual Bailón) is the patron of cooks in Mexico and elsewhere because of a legend that an angel attended to his cooking duties while he prayed before the Eucharist.

Be that as it may, we find no place in this pattern into which Jesús Malverde can fit comfortably. His followers may think he acts like a saint, but what we know of his life (if indeed he existed) has nothing in common with the stories of the saints of the Catholic Church. Saint Dismas was indeed a thief, but he acknowledged Christ as the Messiah when they both were dying. He became a saint in spite of, rather than because of, his thievery. Malverde is quite different: At least in part, his very separation from the law-abiding world gives him his appeal. But he is real to his followers, and his cult is a reality in the world in which we all live.

Saint Anthony (San Antonio) was a Franciscan born in 1221. He was a stirring preacher and wonder-worker, and toiled on behalf of the poor. He is a doctor of the Church.

Saint Cajetan (San Cayetano), a sixteenth-century Italian, founded a low-interest pawnshop to aid the poor. Possibly for this help in raising ready cash, he is popularly considered patron of gamblers. Thus his alleged inability to turn down a wager.

Pancho Villa on horseback, from a prayer card purchased in Texas.

CHAPTER 5

PANCHO VILLA

Bandit, Revolutionary, Hero, Villain—& Saint?

Francisco Villa nació
con el valor mexicano,
para ayudar a los pobres
contra el yugo del tirano.

Francisco Villa was born
with Mexican courage,
to help the poor
against the yoke of tyrants.

—from the corrido "General Francisco Villa"

THE MAN

By far the best known of the folk saints discussed in this book is the famous bandit and revolutionary general Pancho Villa. A recent biography, itself 985 pages long, contains forty-five pages of archival and bibliographic references. Both as a historical and a legendary figure, Villa has played an important role in the western U.S.–Mexico borderlands—a role that shows few signs of ending. We know that he was born Doroteo

Arango in 1878 to a family of sharecroppers on the Rancho de la Coyotada. This in turn belonged to one of the largest haciendas in Durango, the property of the López Negrete family. Around the age of sixteen, Doroteo became a bandit and remained at least close to this occupation in Durango and later in Chihuahua until the 1910 Revolution, when he joined Francisco I. Madero's successful revolution against the elderly dictator Porfirio Díaz. Then, after Madero had become president and was assassinated on the orders of General Victoriano Huerta, Villa revolted against Huerta and, using Chihuahua as a base of operations, gathered troops and started toward Mexico City. He eventually formed the famed División del Norte, quite possibly the most effective fighting force ever assembled in Mexico.

In 1914, he broke with Venustiano Carranza, who styled himself First Chief of Mexico, and Villa's fortunes began their slow decline. After a series of defeats and retreats, he finally surrendered to the Mexican government in 1920 and received amnesty and a ranch—El Canutillo, near Parral, Chihuahua. He was assassinated in the latter city on July 20, 1923, by a group of enemies, supported by at least some factions within the Mexican government. Soon after his death and burial, his body was exhumed by persons unknown and his head removed. To this day nobody knows where it is. Finally, in 1976, President Luis Echevarría had Villa's remains exhumed again and brought to Mexico City, then re-interred there in the Monument of the Revolution.

The Legend

Comenzaron a echar expediciones	They started to send out expeditions
los aeroplanos comenzaron a volar	the airplanes started to fly
por distintas y varias direcciones	in distinct and several directions
buscando a Villa, queriéndolo a matar.	looking for Villa, wishing to kill him.

Los de a caballo ya no se podían sentar	Those on horseback couldn't sit down any more,
mas los de a pie no podían caminar,	and those on foot couldn't walk,
entonces Villa les pasa en aeroplano	then Villa passes them in an airplane
y desde arriba les dijo "Gud bai."	and from above he told them "Good-bye."

–from "La Persecución de Villa," as I learned it from older singers in the 1950s

So much for the facts in skeletal form. Anyone wishing to know more about this fascinating man and his equally interesting era should go to Friedrich Katz' 1998 biography, the most thorough treatment yet of Villa and the source of much of the information in this chapter. The Pancho Villa with whom this chapter is concerned, however, is not the Villa of fact but the Villa of legend—the man whose fame lives on in the hearts and minds of the poor people of northern Mexico. Here, in brief outline, is the Villa legend—or rather, two versions of that legend, one casting Villa as hero and one as villain.

When Doroteo Arango was sixteen, the owner of the hacienda where the Villa family lived demanded Villa's sister as a sleeping partner. Infuriated by this attack upon the family honor, Doroteo shot the offender in the foot and began his life of banditry. At one point or another he was a follower of the famous bandit chiefs Heraclio Bernal and Ignacio Parra. During this phase of his career he changed his name to Francisco Villa, possibly after an earlier, famous local bandit. ("Pancho" is one of several accepted nicknames for "Francisco.") After a while he moved to Chihuahua and started business as a butcher, selling cattle that he and others had stolen. All during this time he distributed money and help to the poor. When the 1910 Revolution started, he was invited to become a follower of Francisco I. Madero and was instrumental in the capture of Ciudad Juárez, just across the border from El Paso, Texas. After General Victoriano Huerta had Madero assassinated and then supplanted him as president of Mexico, Villa joined the revolt against Huerta. He built his División del Norte into an invincible fighting force, with his specially chosen *Dorados* or "Golden Ones" at its core. A consummate strategist and inspirational leader of men, Villa captured the towns of Torreón and Zacatecas, but Carranza prevented him from capturing Mexico City.

Villa then rebelled against Carranza, a rebellion that intensified when he saw that his enemy was not interested in implementing land reforms and helping the poor. Villa's troops, joined by those of Emiliano Zapata, occupied Mexico City and forced Carranza to flee the capital. At this point the famous photograph was taken of Villa occupying the presidential chair in the National Palace, with Zapata sitting next to him.

Villa's triumph, however, was short-lived. Carranza's brilliant general Álvaro Obregón remained faithful to Carranza and fought Villa. Defeated by Obregón's superior generalship in the battles of Celaya and León, Villa retreated north to Chihuahua and tried from there to invade Sonora. He had always been a friend to the United States, until that country betrayed him by helping Carranza move troops to Sonora via the United States, to counter a move by Villa. As a result of that action, Villa murdered several American miners in Chihuahua and engineered a raid on Columbus, New Mexico, on March 9, 1916. This led to the United States' punitive expedition into Chihuahua, led by General Pershing, which in turn reinstated Villa as a hero in the eyes of the Mexican people.

Pancho Villa finally tired of fighting and asked for and received amnesty for himself and his troops from President Aldolfo de la Huerta. He settled down with his followers in the hacienda of El Canutillo in northern Durango, where he lived the useful life of a cattleman and agriculturalist until his assassination.

Many perceive him as a friend of the poor and a deflator of the wealthy and powerful. He distributed some land, especially in Chihuahua, to individuals previously dispossessed by the great cattle and mining interests of that state. In one famous incident, he gathered a number of street urchins in

Mexico City and had them sent to Chihuahua by train to be educated. His murderous rages are admitted, but many feel he killed only those who betrayed him. He made Pershing and his well-equipped army look silly, thus pulling a few tail feathers out of the American eagle. He was a consummate horseman, great general, fearless warrior, implacable enemy, insatiable womanizer, and friend to the downtrodden. *¡Viva Villa, el Centauro del Norte!*

There exists another set of Villa legends, however, which paint Villa as an unredeemed and unredeemable villain. Many of the people who believe, repeat, and act on these stories are descended from those who suffered at Villa's hands. Villa was, in fact, a ruthless, implacable enemy to those he disliked or distrusted. He was also famous for the murder of large numbers of people. During the so-called Villista Terror in Mexico City in 1915, he had numerous members of the upper classes either shot or held for ransom. He routinely executed prisoners—or instructed his murderous henchmen, Rodolfo Fierro and Tomás Urbina, to do so. (In truth, killing prisoners was fairly standard practice for all sides in the Revolution.) When Villa was retreating from Sonora after a 1916 defeat, some men from the Sonoran village of San Pedro de la Cueva fired in exasperation on some of Villa's troops, thinking they were just another bunch of bandits. In retaliation, Villa had all or most of the adult males in the village shot, including the priest, whom he personally executed. And on January 10, 1916, one of Villa's officers stopped a train carrying eighteen American mining engineers and the mine manager back to their mine and had all save one escapee shot. Villa was blamed widely for this atrocity.

Villa, his detractors will tell you, was never much of a general. His only tactic was the all-out cavalry charge, which earned him resounding defeats against Obregón's entrenched machine-gun positions. He was not a revolutionary, but rather a bandit and a mass murderer, plain and simple.

Which of these views represents the historic Villa? Probably both. Villa was a complex man who lived in and responded to brutal times in his country's history. But in Mexico and especially in the border country, it is still difficult to be neutral concerning this larger-than-life figure. In the case of Pancho Villa, one pays one's money and takes one's choice. And many of those choices remain powerful right up to the present day.

When the government of Mexico offered the City of Tucson a huge equestrian statue of Villa, a serious controversy ignited. (The statue was accepted and stands in Tucson in the old downtown district. Its

The spot on the street in Parral, Chihuahua, where Pancho Villa was assassinated. (January 2002)

twin stands at the southern entrance to Parral, Chihuahua.) I have been told by some Tucsonans that Villa was a bandit and a terrorist; for others he was a revolutionary hero and a symbol of resistance to an oppressive system. The man who guided me around the Museo de General Francisco Villa in Parral was a "true believer" in Villa; he informed me that Villa's old Hacienda El Canutillo in Durango, also a museum, was being permitted to deteriorate because the current governor of Durango was an anti-Villista. When I asked him why this might be, he replied that the man's family had doubtless owned property that Villa had confiscated. To some extent social class determines one's opinions on Villa to this day.

But not entirely. After Villa was killed, the custom began among some of his old Dorados of journeying to the site of his murder on July 20, the anniversary of his assassination. In 1994, this custom became institutionalized into a *Jornada Villista,* a civic celebration lasting for several days. Originally, a group of horsemen, many dressed in revolutionary-period costume, rode from Villa's Hacienda El Canutillo to Parral, where a re-enactment of Villa's assassination, funeral, and burial was held. Booths sold traditional foods, groups performed regional dances, and at least some of Villa's famous victories were re-enacted.

The celebration became an annual one, with the civic and political leaders of Parral participating. One year, the cavalcade, dubbed the *gran cabalgata Villista*, rode from Chihuahua City to Parral—or, as some Parraleños put it, "from the capital of the state to the capital of the world." As is customary in Mexican civic celebrations, a queen—in this case, she is called *La Adelita*, after the archetypical revolutionary *soldadera*—is elected. Everyone—or at least everyone so inclined—seems to have a fine time.

So Villa can be said to live on in a number of ways in the great open country of northwestern Mexico, which was his setting. He lives as a historical character, and one who can still excite controversy and even passionate dispute. But he also lives on as a spiritual helper for many who perceive themselves as being given an unfair deal in this world.

PRAYERS TO PANCHO VILLA

Katz devotes one paragraph toward the end of his monumental work to Villa as an object of posthumous religious devotion. I first became aware of Villa as a religious figure in August 1994, when I purchased a prayer card from a Tucson florist who also sells religious articles. The card is printed in black ink on heavy, tan-colored card stock. One side shows a well-groomed Villa wearing a coat and tie and is labeled: AUTENTICA ORACION AL ESPIRITU DE PANCHO VILLA ("Authentic Prayer to the Spirit of Pancho Villa"). On the other side is printed:

ORACION al Espíritu Mártir de Pancho Villa, Gran General Revolucionario. En el nombre de Dios Nuestro Señor invoco a los espíritus que te protejan para que me ayudes. Así como ayudastes en el mundo terrenal a los NECESITADOS. Así como venciste a los PODEROSOS. Así como hiciste retroceder a tus ENIMIGOS. Así te pido tu protección espiritual, para que me libres de todo mal y me des el ánimo necesario y el valor suficiente para enfrentarme a lo más difícil que se me presente en la vida. Amén.

Rece esta oración 9 días seguidos con fé al caer la tarde. Y Consérvela siempre al lado del corazón para su protección.

(PRAYER to the Martyred Spirit of Pancho Villa, Great Revolutionary General. In the name of God our Lord, I invoke the spirits that protect you, that you may help me. Just as you helped the NEEDY in this earthly world. Just as you conquered the POWERFUL. Just as you made your ENEMIES fall back. Thus I ask your spiritual protection, that you may free me from all evil and give me the necessary courage and enough bravery to face the greatest difficulty that is sent me in this life. Amen. Pray this 9 consecutive days faithfully as it grows dark. And keep it on the side of your heart for your protection.)

An unusual portrait of Villa with coat and tie.

I have since purchased eleven other Pancho Villa cards in Ciudad Juárez and in south Texas. Eight carry this same prayer, although each shows a different image of Villa on the front. I've seen Villa in military uniform, several poses of Villa on horseback, and Villa in Stetson and crossed bandoliers. Surprisingly enough, there is even a drawing of Villa in crossed bandoliers and a charro hat—a piece of headwear not commonly associated with him. (The wide, dish-brimmed, embroidered charro hat is more usually associated with Emiliano Zapata, the great agrarian leader.) Two cards have no printed material at all on their backs (one shows yet a different sketch of Villa in coat and tie), while one, showing the hero in a Stetson hat, bears a brief biography but no prayers. All were purchased in *yerberías* or stores specializing in herbs and religious items, especially those used in *curanderismo*.

A final Pancho Villa card shows the general on horseback, and is labeled GENERAL PANCHO VILLA, THE MAN WHO DARED INVADE THE U.S.A. The prayer on the back of this card reads:

ORACION AL ESPIRITU DE PANCHO VILLA

Querido hermano, tú que supiste vencer a tus más fieros enemigos, haz que triunfe en mis más difíciles empresas.

Me socorras en mi negocio y penalidades; a ti invoco de todo corazón, así pues, te sirvas darme valor, tú que fuiste guía de los desamparados y sufridos, dadme tu pensamiento y tu osadía. Así sea.

Se rezan tres Padres Nuestros y tres Ave Marias.

("Prayer to the spirit of Pancho Villa.

Beloved brother, you who knew how to conquer your fiercest enemies, cause me to triumph in my most difficult undertakings.

Help me in my occupation and in my hardships; I invoke you with all my heart, thus, you give me bravery, you who were guide of the abandoned and suffering ones, give me your thought and your daring. May it be so.

One prays three Our Fathers and three Hail Marys.")

This prayer appears on two cards.

Of the printed Villa representations I have discussed, most are done in black and white, apparently the products of anonymous, possibly small, print shops. The card with the biographical material was produced by "Ediciones BOB, S.A." and is labeled "No. 1547." One pocket-sized color representation that carries the "standard prayer" was actually printed in Italy—in fact, Villa's face on this card has a somewhat Italian character! A final prayer appears on one side of an 8½"x 6½" piece of paper with a printed frame around it. It was printed by a Mexico City company, "Cromos y Novedades de Mexico, S.A. de C.V."

The prayers are quite practical; they ask Villa dead to do what the living Villa of legend was famous for—stand up for the underdog and confound his oppressors. They request the gift of bravery in the face of seemingly insurmountable troubles. None of the prayers speaks of intercession; all, as is so common in Mexican folk Catholicism, ask the figure addressed for direct assistance. An interesting touch is the reference to "the spirits that protect you" in the standard prayer. This moves us into the second aspect of what one might call the cult of Pancho Villa. Not only do his followers approach him for favors and help as though he were a saint, they also deal directly with him through mediums believed to be in contact with the spirit world.

PANCHO VILLA AS SPIRIT

In 1953 the anthropologist Isabel Kelly did field work on the traditional healing beliefs and systems of the Laguna area of the state of Coahuila, in and near the city of Torreón. I should note that two of Villa's most famous battles took place in Torreón, which during his lifetime was considered one of the geographic cores of his support. So it shouldn't surprise us that here, some thirty years after his murder, anthropologists encountered mediums who consulted his spirit.

Kelly does not devote much time to Villa's spirit. She does mention a young man with a nervous disorder, cured when Villa's spirit drove from his body the evil spirits that had possessed him by liberal use of a whip and "not very acceptable language." In another place, Kelly says that her Spiritualist informants mentioned Villa fairly frequently. She describes him as "a popular hero whose picturesque language so embarrasses the assembled company that the operator of one spiritualistic center has the group pray, asking that the offending spirit withdraw and not return." On another occasion, Villa's spirit advised a man trying to validate his claim to a certain piece of property. The man asked his wife, a spiritualistic medium, to consult the spirit of Villa "whom he knew well and who was a good businessman." Pancho Villa dictated a letter that the medium, who was illiterate, typed for him, the petitioner obtained the signature of the lawyer Villa had recommended, and he gained title to the property.

I have also been told that Villa's spirit sometimes descends on *Fidencista materias,* or mediums who channel the spirit of El Niño Fidencio, as explained in Chapter 7. On these occasions, my informant tells me, if the person being cured is a woman, she does well to be cautious. Even though the mediums are mostly women, when they are taken over by Pancho Villa's spirit, one should watch out—he is a "groper"! This is, of course, perfectly in line with Villa's reputation during his lifetime as an enthusiastic womanizer.

Anthropologist Ruth Behar has encountered and written about Pancho Villa in spirit form. In her book *Translated Woman: Crossing the Border with Esperanza's Story,* she describes in great detail a séance in which a medium takes on Villa's persona. It happened in San Luís Potosí, on Pancho (Francisco) Villa's saint's day—October 4, the day of St. Francis of Assisi. She, her *comadre* Esperanza, and a number of other people assembled in the medium's house, which contained an altar room. The congregation brought offerings for the feast that would take place, as well as presents for Villa—packets of cigarettes and bottles of tequila, both of the cheapest brands, "because the general despised anything too refined." The offerings also included a three-layer iced cake, with *"Felicidades Pancho Villa"* written on it. It sat on a stool through the first parts of the ceremony.

The medium, a very masculine-appearing woman, went into a trance almost immediately. The first spirit to appear was that of Amalia Díaz de Bonilla, one of Villa's many wives. She announced that the general was looking forward to his birthday party and then made room for Villa

I have in my files two prayer cards titled *Oración al Todopoderoso e invocación al espíritu puro de* Tomasito Herrera (Prayer to the Almighty and invocation of the pure spirit of Tommy Herrera). The prayer asks Almighty God to permit the pure spirit of Tomasito, along with the petitioner's Guardian Angel, to be the petitioner's protector. An obviously doctored photograph of a rather odd-looking little boy is labeled TOMASITO HERRERA, ESPÍRITU DE MÁS ALLÁ ("Tommy Herrera, spirit from farther along"). My depictions of Tomasito were all purchased in south Texas.

himself, who spoke through the medium in a deep voice. The people sang the Mexican national anthem and las mañanitas, the birthday song, to him. Villa then commanded everyone to march in place, faster and faster. After some call-and-response in which they reaffirmed their identity as Pancho Villa's soldiers, a roll call was taken. Then people who had previously been cured by the General gave their testimonies, describing their previous ailments or problems, and the ways in which they were cured. As each one came forward, he or she was *entregado*—received—by Villa, who assured them that they would find the reliefs they sought. He often spoke "in the name of the Father, the Son, Amen." (But apparently not in the name of the Holy Spirit, which would be expected in a more Catholic situation.)

Then the fiesta began, with meat in *mole* sauce, rice, tortillas, and bottled soda. Everyone present had one or more helpings of the rich food, including the three-tiered cake. Then came more consultations, more testimonies, more words of help and advice from Villa. Finally, everyone shook hands with their neighbors, and Villa's spirit was sent back to the spirit world. The session continued, however, with the brief appearance of the spirit of Tomasito, a little boy, after which most of the participants left. Then followed a complicated series of events in which several of the people who remained were requested by the medium to display imaginary possessions or even to grind imaginary corn. Finally, all was over, and everyone went home.

LA TUMBA DE VILLA

Parral is still Villista country in a number of ways. Villa is often quoted as having said that he wanted to stay in Parral until his death. It was in Parral that the Pershing expedition met serious resistance from an angry mob. Parraleños placed and maintained crosses for years at Villa's death site. And Villa was buried in the Parral cemetery until his removal for re-internment in Mexico City. Some say he's still there.

According to one story, some time after Villa's death a young woman dying of cancer arrived in Parral, on her way to Chihuahua City, where she had been sent by doctors in Zacatecas, in hopes of a cure. She was so weak that she could not continue her journey past Parral. After she died, those who went through her possessions could find no clue to her identity—only a large sum of money. This was spent in securing elaborate Masses in Parral's several churches and in having her buried near Villa's grave in the Panteón Dolores. A plain black cross of pipe was erected at the head of her grave.

However, she wasn't in that grave at all. Villa family members and supporters had taken the opportunity to disinter the

Small case of ex-votos and Villa's death mask at his tomb in Parral, Chihuahua. (January 2002)

general's remains and place them in the grave of the unknown young woman, while her body was placed in Villa's grave. Thus further desecration of Villa's body would be avoided. Decades later, when the president of Mexico sent an Army officer to disinter Villa's skeleton and carry it to Mexico City, a doctor in attendance told the officer that the body he had couldn't possibly be that of Pancho Villa. "No matter," replied the officer— "My orders were to remove the body from this grave and I'm following my orders!" The purpose of this complex narrative seems clear—it proves to all who wish to believe it that Pancho Villa is still in his beloved Parral. After all, we were told, Villa said that he wanted to live in Parral, to die in Parral, and to be in Parral forever. Thus his wish was fulfilled.

On January 20, 2002, Alfredo Gonzales and I visited Pancho Villa's tomb in Panteón Dolores in Parral. A man approached our car and tried to sell us a commemorative coin. He then alerted an elderly, limping caretaker, who escorted us at a dignified pace to the rear of the cemetery where Villa's tomb stands. The tomb itself has changed over the years. In one version of the story, some time after the removal of Villa's skull, a cement slab was poured over the grave to discourage further desecration. The monument got more and more elaborate, until today's tomb consists of a paved area perhaps twenty feet square. It is backed by a high cement wall, and surrounded on the other three sides by a green cement wall perhaps two feet high, surmounted by a yellow iron fence with wagon wheels inserted in it. A sliding gate protects the entire area. A vertical slab on the right side of the high wall holds a reproduction of Villa's death mask and the legend "FRANCISCO VILLA, 1878–1923." A metal plaque perhaps three feet square relates details of Villa's career.

Set into the pavement of the tomb are three memorial stones. The top one reads GRAL. FRANCISCO VILLA, PARRAL, 20 DE JULIO DE 1923. 1936-SEPTIEMBRE. LOS INSULTOS Y SUS AUTORES NO RENPLAZARAN AL GUERRERO EN LOS BRAZOS DE LA HISTORIA Y SI EXHIBEN SU BAJEZA. GRAL. JUAN N. MEDINA. [This translates to "The insults and their authors will not replace the warrior in the embrace of History, and they do reveal their baseness."] The middle one reads PRESENTE MI GENERAL. CORONEL RAMÓN CORDOVA SAENZ. The lower one reads PRESENTE MI GENERAL. CORL. J. M. JAURRIETA. DIC. 1948. As in life, Villa remains in the company of loyal followers.

A small three-sided metal case is attached to the large vertical slab. Its front is barred, and it contains photographs of Villa, one small plaster statue of the general on a rearing horse, and several ex-votos. One woman from Monterrey, Nuevo León, apparently left copies of her education diploma and a number of teachers' excellence certificates, all framed together with the legend "Gracias, General Francisco Villa." Several individual photos are framed separately. A business card from an employee of Seguros Monterrey Aetna (the Monterrey branch of the Aetna insurance company) is slipped partially behind another piece of paper. On it is written in pencil *estoy presente, general* ("I am here, general").

There is one longer ex-voto, dated July 19, 1998, and signed by a grandmother, mother, and daughter, all from Monterrey. (This city, incidentally, is known as an important Spiritualist center.) Its legend reads "DOY GRACIAS PRIMERAMENTE A DIOS NUESTRO SEÑOR JESUCRISTO Y A FRANCISCO VILLA Y A TODOS LOS SANTOS QUE AYUDARON A SACARME ADE-LANTE EN MI ENFERMIDAD QUE __ MENOS DE TRES MESES TUVE MI ALIVIA Y HASTA LA FECHA ME HAN AYUDADO EN PROBLEMAS RESOLVER Y USTEDES LOS HAN RESOLVADOS. POR ESO LES DOY GRACIAS POR TODO. ESTAMOS MUY AGRADECIDOS. " ("I give thanks first to God, our Lord Jesus Christ, and to Francisco Villa and all the saints who helped bring me out of a sickness, from which in less than three months I felt better, and up to now you have helped me to resolve problems and you have resolved them. For that I give thanks for all. We are very grateful.")

We asked the elderly cemetery caretaker who took us to Villa's grave about the story of the two tombs recounted earlier. He replied that he'd heard it, but didn't pay it much attention. Referring to Villa's grave, he told us, "Some say it's there" (pointing in one direction) "and some say it's over there" (pointing in the opposite direction), "but when I came here twenty-seven years ago, it was right here!" (pointing at the official tomb).

SOCIAL BANDITS & SAINTS

So Pancho Villa, like Jesús Malverde, is considered by at least some people to be, or rather to behave like, a saint. The chances of either man being officially recognized as such by the Catholic Church seem to be non-existent. Both were bandits in periods of great social and economic inequality and oppression. Malverde died a bandit, while Villa became a world-famous revolutionary general.

But they were more than bandits; they were "social bandits." According to bandit authority Eric Hobsbawm, social bandits are "peasant outlaws whom the lord and state regard as criminals, and who are considered by their people as heroes, champions, as avengers, fighters for justice, perhaps even leaders of liberation, and in any case as men to be admired, helped, and supported." This fits both Villa in his earlier days and Malverde as he is described in oral tradition. Both men are said to have been motivated by revenge; both "robbed from the rich" (who, after all, are the most practical targets for robbery). Villa stole cattle belonging to Chihuahua's powerful Terrazas family; Malverde held up stages. Each is reputed to have, in some way, "given to the poor." In each case, the poor have reciprocated by bestowing a form of immortality upon their deceased benefactor. Although nobody seems to suggest that either Malverde or Villa will return, King Arthur-like, to help their people in their time of need, each man remains active after death, interceding with God on behalf of the powerless or visiting them in the form of a spirit, giving advice and encouragement.

This sort of thing is not unique to Mexico or new to Catholic tradition. Dismas, the first saint, was a thief, but he entered heaven because he repented on the cross and recognized Christ as the Son of God. Not all criminals are social bandits, of course, and we have no evidence that Dismas before his conversion experience was anything but a common thief (or perhaps an uncommon one, since he got caught). But his story offers at least one bit of evidence that Mediterranean Catholics (and Mexican Catholicism sprang from a Mediterranean transplant) have venerated the memory of bandits, and possibly of social bandits, since the early days of Christianity. Precedents for popular devotions to such figures as Villa and Malverde do exist.

We find one example in a biography of St. Martin of Tours, written around A.D. 400 by Sulpicius Severus. It tells how, when the saint became bishop of Tours, he was curious concerning an altar outside of the town, said to have been placed over the grave of an early Christian martyr. When questioning the older members of the community, St. Martin was unable to obtain any clear narrative concerning the martyr, or his or her circumstances of martyrdom. So he went out to the altar with several of his companions, and, standing over the grave, he prayed that God might reveal to him the identity of the individual buried there.

A "loathsome and fierce shadow" immediately appeared at his left side. When St. Martin demanded to know the shadow's identity, it replied that it had been a brigand who had been executed for his misdeeds. After death, the spirit had deceived the common folk into believing that he was a saint in glory rather than a sinner undergoing punishment. This suggests that, as early as the fourth century, a gap between the Catholicism of the Church and the Catholicism of the people existed.

Coming closer to us in time and space, the inhabitants of Querétaro in the late eighteenth century revered portraits of a local man who had been sentenced to death just as though he were a saint. These are only some examples I have stumbled across in the course of my reading; I have no doubt that there are many more. It would seem that the common folk in the Catholic world have been venerating bandits and other less-than-respectable individuals for a very long time.

From a prayer card to
Don Pedrito Jaramillo.

CHAPTER 6

DON PEDRITO

God's Humble Helper in South Texas

*Se sabe que hay una historia
de la que escribo muy poquito
del hombre que alcanzó GLORIA
su nombre es: "TATA PEDRITO"*

–from "Tata Pedrito, Razgos Biográficos, Versificados" by Liborio Rodriguez

It is known that there is a story
about which I'm writing very little
of the man who reached HEAVEN
whose name is GRANDPA PEDRITO

THE MAN

His real name was Pedro Jaramillo. The "Don," which almost always precedes his Christian name, is a title of respect, while the diminutive "Pedrito," almost invariably used for this remarkable man, indicates affection. He was born into poverty near Guadalajara, Jalisco, Mexico, in or about the year 1829. He made his living as a laborer. According to one version of his legend, one day Pedro was hit on the nose by a branch while riding through the brush. This injury became very painful, and one night when he could not sleep he went out to a nearby wallow and plastered mud on his nose. This relieved the pain and allowed him to sleep. While he slept, God appeared to him and told him to dedicate his life to healing the sick and injured. He carried the scar on his nose to his grave. The biographical poem I just quoted tells a slightly different version. It has Pedrito suffering an unnamed accident and lying on the ground for three days, wounded in the head and surrounded by poisonous snakes. The men who found him were sure he was either dead or dying, when suddenly a horse appeared, killed the snakes, and saved Don Pedrito's life. This could only have been an act of Divine Providence, we are told, for not even science could have saved the life of the holy man.

Another legend relates that, when his mother became very ill, Don Pedrito prayed for her recovery, saying that if she died he would leave Mexico forever. When she died he kept his promise and crossed the border into Texas, settling on Los Olmos ("The Elms") ranch, near present-day Falfurrias. This was in 1881. It is said that he knew this region from an earlier trip when he and a friend had brought liquor from Mexico to a local rancher for his annual Día de San Juan celebration.

Upon his arrival at Los Olmos, Don Pedrito immediately established himself as a curandero. He refused to charge for his cures, but would accept money if it were offered. This money he mostly spent on food and supplies

DON PEDRITO JARAMILLO

Portrait of Don Pedrito, from a prayer card.

for the people who began to flock to him for help. During the terrible drought of the early 1890s, he is said to have fed hundreds of poor folks—and had to hire a cook and another helper to assist him. All the money for this came from free-will donations. Much of the necessary food he grew himself on a hundred-acre plot of land given him by a neighbor.

As many as five hundred people at a time were said to have camped at Los Olmos Creek, waiting for a chance to see Don Pedrito. Whole families would accompany a sick relative…and all these people had to be fed. Supplies he could not grow himself were hauled by wagon from the nearby town of Alice (Falfurrias was not established until the arrival of the railroad in 1903, four years before Don Pedrito's death.) At one time he ordered a whole barrel of cube sugar—a substance that featured in some of his prescriptions. As many as two hundred letters a week requesting help and advice began pouring in, and the Paisano Post Office was established at Los Olmos at some point after his arrival. By the time of his death in 1907, Don Pedrito Jaramillo was easily the best-known and most-loved individual in all of south Texas.

THE CURES

Siempre, siempre que curaba	Always, always when he cured
invocaba al REDENTOR;	he invoked the REDEEMER;
y el que sufría, ya confiaba	and he who suffered had faith
no sentir mas el dolor.	that he would not suffer
	pain any more.
Nunca cobraba él DINERO,	He never charged MONEY,
ni dádivas reclamaba;	nor asked for gifts to be returned;
en todo fue muy sincero	he was very sincere in everything
y al más enfermo SANABA.	and CURED the sickest person.

Folk Saints of the Borderlands

This selection from a twenty-six-verse poem I purchased at the Don Pedrito shrine touches upon what many people feel to be the salient characteristics of Pedro's career as a curandero. First, he claimed no special powers for himself, but continuously stated that God used him to allow individuals to cure themselves through their own faith. Secondly, he asked for no payments, and thirdly, he was to a great degree successful.

In her 1951 article on Don Pedrito, Ruth Dodson gives a number of accounts of cures that she collected from oral tradition in south Texas. It seems that the curandero would often prescribe some common action or substance, and allow the patient's faith in God a chance to work. I offer a sampling of the cures as told to Dodson:

A man suffering from sunstroke was on his way to Los Olmos from Yorktown, some hundred miles away. When he got to Alice, which was thirty miles from Los Olmos, he found Don Pedrito there, performing cures. After hearing of his problem, Don Pedrito told him to go off by himself and bathe for nine consecutive days. The man persuaded Don Pedro to accept $25 as a gift, then started for home. On the way, he camped for nine days near a water tank, bathing himself daily. He arrived home in excellent health, and remained grateful into his old age, many years later.

A young girl had a swelling on her neck, and her family took her by wagon from Corpus Christi, a journey of some sixty miles, to see Don Pedrito. While they were awaiting their turn at Los Olmos, Don Pedrito ministered to a woman who had seizures believed to be a result of witchcraft. Don Pedrito was unable to cure this woman, who failed to respond to his treatment during a seizure. The family subsequently learned that she later fell into a fire and died as a result of burns. But he told the parents of the little girl to buy a bottle of inexpensive olive oil and rub the soles of her feet with it, toe to heel, using a chicken feather. This they were to do for nine consecutive nights, which they did upon their return home, and the child was cured.

Not only Mexicanos were helped by Don Pedrito. The postmaster at Paisano, who also taught school at Los Olmos, had a young daughter suffering terribly from a toothache, so much so that she could not sleep at night. Don Pedrito told her to roast a clove of garlic and put it in her shoe, on the foot opposite from the side where the toothache was, and to keep the shoe on all night. She followed instructions, and the family set off on the thirty-mile trip to a dentist, to get the tooth pulled. After a painful day of travel, the child spread a blanket out on the ground and immediately fell asleep. When she awoke in the morning, the pain was gone. They did not go to the dentist, and the tooth came painlessly out in pieces a few days later, just as Don Pedrito had predicted.

This same girl returned from a visit to an aunt in Louisiana in a very nervous condition. Don Pedrito prescribed that she bathe in a tub of water at daybreak for three successive mornings and that her mother make her a sleeveless jacket of new unbleached muslin that she should not take off for nine days. After this was done, the girl regained her health. Interestingly enough, when the mother herself asked for a cure, Don Pedrito refused her, saying that she did not have sufficient faith.

Various other prescriptions included a poultice of canned tomatoes for a pain in the side, nine baths for a leg injury, and halves of a roasted lemon tied to the soles of the feet. The mother of a lad with nosebleed was told to put clean clothes on her son and not change them for nine days. Each night she should pour a bucket of water over the boy, thoroughly wetting him, and he should sleep that way. An epileptic was to go into her yard for nine consecutive nights, lift her eyes to heaven, say "In the name of God," drink one swallow of water, and throw the rest out. All these remedies resulted in the desired cures.

Certain patterns emerge from the accounts of Don Pedrito's cures. He seems to have prescribed whatever came to his mind or was easily at hand. As he so often repeated, it was not he or his actions that did the curing, but rather God working through the faith of the individual. Many of his treatments were to be repeated nine times—the number of days in a Catholic novena. Three, that pervasive quantity in European thought and custom both sacred and secular, formal and informal, also appears frequently in Don Pedrito's instructions.

Don Pedrito also had clairvoyant powers that allowed him to know things without being told. One man doubted that the prescribed cure would work. Don Pedrito told him: "I am as sure that this remedy will cure you as I am that you are wearing a pair of borrowed shoes." The shoes were in fact borrowed, and the man believed and was cured. Another man pretended an ailment in order to test Don Pedrito. Don Pedrito advised him to eat a bale of hay and then said, "When one brings a lie, he will take a lie."

Some of the stories concerning Don Pedrito's cures are both practical and amusing. A man in Mexico drank hastily from a pond of water and got a grass burr stuck in his throat. He went to several doctors, who told him that it could only be removed surgically. He didn't want an operation and was suffering terribly. He had heard of Don Pedrito in Texas, so he went to visit him. The curandero told him to drink all that he could of water with salt in it. When he did so, he became nauseated and vomited up the grass burr, which by that time had sprouted two little leaves. Another woman had recurring migraine headaches. When someone went to Don Pedrito on her behalf, the curandero instructed that her head be cut off and fed to the hogs. When the woman heard this, she became violently angry...and her headaches ceased.

Don Pedrito, the Medical Profession & the Church

As we have seen, Teresita Urrea, roughly a contemporary of Don Pedrito's, was viewed with deep reservations by the clergy and the medical profession. Such was apparently not the case with Don Pedrito. There are probably several reasons for this difference. South Texas was not under a centralized, conservative, authoritarian regime like Mexico's Porfiriato. It was still a frontier region, sparsely and recently settled, and while most

Mexicans had little political, social, or economic power in the largely Anglo-American establishment, they were to a great extent left to themselves by that establishment. While Teresita was courted by revolutionaries and Spiritualists, each of which groups had its own agenda, Don Pedrito seems to have been left alone with his people. No doubt this was another function of his isolation.

One well-known doctor, a contemporary of Don Pedrito's, believed Don Pedrito to be an intelligent but uneducated man, who in fact cured many people. When it was suggested to him that the curandero be prohibited from practicing, he said, "No, how do I know that Don Pedrito's prayers don't do more good than my pills?" We can find accounts of legal investigations of Don Pedrito for practicing medicine without a license, but as he made no charges for his services, nothing was done.

Don Pedrito was always careful to say that God was the one who worked the cures. During much of Don Pedrito's life, the local priest was a Frenchman, Father Peter Bard. Stationed in the small town of San Diego, in Duval County, Texas, Father Bard covered a large part of south Texas, bringing the sacraments to the people who otherwise would have no contact with the Church. He seems to have respected Don Pedrito as a gentle man who worked in the service of humanity. When one of his altar boys spoke disparagingly of Don Pedrito and his remedies, Father Bard responded that "God, knowing of the great need of the people where there were so few doctors, saw fit to bestow on this humble man the power of helping these people. He had endowed him for the work. And the servant fulfilled his vocation faithfully."

When the town of Falfurrias was founded in 1903 with the arrival of the railroad, a Catholic church was built with materials and labor contributed by several local men. Needing money to buy a bell for the new church, the group appointed a local man to try to raise the necessary funds. The first person he approached was Don Pedrito. He was also the last, for the elderly curandero offered to give a sum of up to $1,500 for the project. The bell was purchased and used for years.

Representatives of the Church still seem to approve of Don Pedrito, but with some reservations. A pamphlet printed in 1972 quotes a "local church bulletin" as follows: "It is common knowledge that 'Don Pedro,' the famous healer of nearby Los Olmos, did much good and helped many persons in his life. We must remember that Don Pedro is not a recognized saint of the church. Therefore, he cannot be given veneration like that shown St. Martin or St. Jude. Statues should not be bought for use in home shrines." The same source states that at least one local priest felt that some individuals encouraged belief in Don Pedrito for reasons of personal gain.

DON PEDRITO'S SPIRIT TODAY

Adiós, hermano Pedrito,	Farewell, brother Pedrito,
échanos tu bendición	give your blessing
a todos estos hermanos	to all these brothers and sisters
que estamos en la reunión,	who are at the meeting,
que estamos en la reunión.	who are at the meeting.
Adios, hermano Pedrito,	Farewell, brother Pedrito
de la ciencia espiritual;	of the spiritual science;
aquí nos quedamos tristes;	saddened we remain;
sabe Dios si volverás,	God knows if you will return,
sabe Dios si volverás.	God knows if you will return.

–verses two and three of "Don Pedrito Jaramillo," sung on the lower Rio Grande at the end of séances with Don Pedrito's spirit

I have little doubt that some people do venerate the deceased curandero as a saint, that prayers are addressed to him, that candles are burned in his honor, and that pictures and statues of him adorn some altars, especially in his traditional territory of south Texas. He is also believed to help in person, channeled by mediums.

By 1926, Don Pedrito's spirit was being called upon for help. In that year a woman was threatened with unjust imprisonment, along with her son. She went to a Spiritualist in San Diego, Texas, and requested to speak with the spirit of Don Pedrito. Don Pedrito assured her that things would come out well, and they did, after four years of court action and appeals. Every day of those four years she prayed that the spirit of Don Pedrito would help them.

By 1948, Don Pedrito's portrait hung in a place of honor in a Spiritualist temple in Monterrey, Mexico, and his was the most popular spirit called upon in that place. By 1953, Don Pedrito's spirit was very popular among Spiritualists living near Torreón, Coahuila. Isabel Kelly, who worked there studying traditional healing practices, noted that Don Pedrito's spirit is celebrated Monterrey and possibly over much of northern Mexico as well. She added that one Torreón medium claimed Don Pedro to have been a lawyer born in Monterrey!

A LOS ANGELES GUARDIANES Y ESPIRITUS PROTECTORES

Espíritus prudentes y benévolos, mensajeros de Dios cuya misión es la de asistir a los hombres y conducir por el buen camino; sostenedme en las pruebas de esta vida, dadme fuerzas para sufrirlas sin murmurar, desviad de mí los malos pensamientos y hacedme que no de acceso a ninguno de los malos Espíritus que intenten inducirme al mal. Iluminad mi conciencia para que pueda ver mis defectos, separad de mis ojos el velo de orgullo que podría impedirme el verlos y digno de vuestra benevolencia. Conocéis mis necesidades; haced pues, que me sea concedida la gracia según la voluntad de Dios.

Vos sobre todo. N_____ mi Angel de la Guarda que velais más particularmente sobre mí y vosotors espíritus protectores que tomáis interés por mí, hacedme que me haga confesármelos a mí mismo

AMEN

ORACION AL TODOPODEROSO Y EVOCACION AL ESPIRITU PURO

D. PEDRITO JARAMILLO

Another prayer card to Don Pedrito.

THE DON PEDRITO SHRINE

Don Pedrito's shrine is located at his grave site near Falfurrias, Texas. It is advertised by a large billboard on each of the two highways that skirt the site. DON PEDRITO SHRINE, proclaims one, with a large red arrow pointing in the appropriate direction. "Take 1418 east one mile." The site itself lies within a small cemetery surrounded by a chain-link fence. A sign by the gate announces that the fence was donated by a couple in Glendale, Arizona. A Texas state historic marker stands outside the fence, giving a brief account of Don Pedrito in English and Spanish. The English version reads:

> DON PEDRO JARAMILLO
> (1830–1907)
> CALLED "THE HEALER OF LOS OLMOS." BORN IN JALISCO, MEXICO. SAID TO HAVE BEEN CURED BY FAITH, THEN GIVEN THE GIFT OF HEALING IN A VISION. HE CAME TO LOS OLMOS RANCH IN 1881. MANY CAME TO HIM BECAUSE, UNLIKE OTHER FAITH HEALERS, HE CLAIMED NO POWER OF HIS OWN, BUT SAID THAT GOD'S HEALING WAS RELEASED THROUGH FAITH. HE MADE NO CHARGES. PATIENTS GAVE WHATEVER THEY CHOSE. BUT WHATEVER WAS GIVEN VOLUNTARILY HE OFTEN GAVE TO THE POOR—FOOD AS WELL AS REMEDIES. HE TRAVELED WIDELY TO VISIT THE SICK. HUNDREDS GAVE TESTIMONIALS OF THEIR HEALINGS.

A cement sidewalk flanked by sturdy rails leads through the cemetery, straight to the front door of the shrine. To one side stands a stone monument with a plaque that states:

> THE JARAMILLO FAMILY CEMETERY
> INSIDE THIS FENCE IS APPROXIMATELY 70 FEET SQUARE. IT WILL NEVER BE INCREASED IN SIZE. AS LONG AS BURIAL SPACE IS AVAILABLE

Highway sign, directing the visitor to Don Pedrito's shrine.

WITHIN THE ENCLOSURE, DIRECT DESCENDANTS OF DON PEDRITO WILL BE BURIED HERE. THEREAFTER, THE CEMETERY WILL BE PRESERVED AS A SHRINE.

The shrine itself is a small, yellowish-white brick building, with a central gable over a door flanked by tall pilasters. It replaces an earlier wooden structure that burned down. A red brick Latin cross in low relief is over the door. The outer appearance of the building led me to expect a church-like interior, with an altar at the end opposite the door and perhaps rows of benches facing the altar. This expectation was only partly fulfilled. A small altar does indeed sit at the far end of the single room, with a crucifix over it and representations of Christ and the Virgin on it, but there is also a door beside it, and it is far from the focal point of the interior space.

The focal point lies to the left of the front door as one enters, and consists of Don Pedrito's grave and headstone. This latter bears his portrait and describes him as a "benefactor of humanity." Between it and the front door stands a life-sized, very solid statue of the seated curandero, painted realistically. In front of the grave sit a kneeler, two rows of benches, and a row of plastic chairs. Behind these in turn I saw a large table covered with a deep layer of sand, with a heat shield and chimney over it. This is for candles. Wreaths line the edge of the ceiling, and photographs of individuals are pinned to cork boards to the right of the door and behind the grave. Many have notes pinned to them. One individual, for example, asked for a good result on medical tests—and a blessing on the doctor and nurses involved—while another asked for a job and security for his family. Discarded crutches are stacked in the corner next to the back door.

Prayer candles for sale at the Don Pedrito Store—including candles to Pancho Villa, the Lost Soul in Purgatory, El Niño Fidencio, and more. (July 2002)

My most recent visit to the shrine was on a Saturday in July 2002. Weekends, according to the shrine's caretakers, are the busiest days at the shrine, with people coming and going all day. (The guest book in the store averaged about ten new signatures per day, although I suspect that many users of the shrine do not sign in.) While we were there, a man, perhaps in his fifties, laid out some plastic bottles on the sand table and vested himself in a white robe with a red sash and red stole. He prayed before the tomb, and then lit incense in a saucepan and waved the pungent smoke around the tomb, the statue, and the altar at the far end of the room. He then seated himself in a chair in a far corner and started to take individual consultations. There were perhaps five people seated in the chapel, with others coming and going. One elderly blind man was led in and prayed before the tomb. Already, at about ten in the morning, the site had seen quite a bit of "action."

A small building signed THE DON PEDRITO STORE stands to the north of the cemetery. It remains in the care of descendants of Don Pedrito's adopted son. A neighbor had died, leaving a large family of children. Don Pedrito offered to adopt one little boy, an offer that was accepted. The son helped Don Pedrito, served as his secretary, and later passed along eyewitness stories of the famous curandero to his own grandchildren.

The store sells photos and statues of Don Pedrito, as well as books about his life and even a printed poem in his honor. It also sells prayer cards addressed to him, asking for his help. While most of the Don Pedrito cards I have seen are printed on cheap paper, one card has a color photograph, laminated in plastic and printed in Italy! Another was produced by a large firm in Mexico City.

The prayers on the cards and sheets vary. One brief prayer, on the back page of a novena to La Santísima Muerte, simply says: *OH! ESPÍRITU PURIFICADO DE DON PEDRITO JARAMILLO, SI TE LO PERMITE AL ALTÍSIMO COMO YO FERVIENTEMENTE LO SUPLICO, ACÉRCATE A MI Y AYÚDAME A CURAR MIS DOLENCIAS* ("Oh! Purified spirit of Don Pedrito Jaramillo, if the Most High allows it as I most fervently beg, come near to me and help me to cure my ailments"). A longer prayer also addresses God and contains the previously quoted prayer within it. A third sheet bears Don Pedrito's photograph,

The Lost Soul in Purgatory is shown in art as an apparently naked woman, with her long hair covering her breasts. She stands chest-deep in flames, with her hands raised in supplication.

La Santísima Muerte ("Most Holy Death") usually appears as a crowned, robed skeleton. Unlike the many playful representations of skeletons associated with Mexico's Day of the Dead, this one seems intended to be terrifying in aspect.

but contains prayers to the Guardian Angel and other angelic and spirit protectors, and a prayer for the medium, that he or she succeed in obtaining the help of good spirits. An 8½"x11" sheet printed by the Don Pedrito Shrine calls on Divine Providence, the Guardian Angel, the individual's spirit guide, protector spirits, and the great Power.

Although Don Pedrito is the subject of most of the materials sold at the store, other figures appear as well. One can, for instance, purchase candles dedicated to Pancho Villa, El Niño Fidencio, the Lost Soul in Purgatory, and La Santisima Muerte, as well as to Don Pedrito. Other, more ominous candles I saw there bore the legends "*Tapabocas*" ("mouth-closer"), "Controlling," and "Law Stay Away."

CURANDERISMO

Don Pedrito Jaramillo was a curandero. Curanderismo is extremely important all over Mexico as well as on the border. So much has been written about traditional healing theory and practice in the Lower Rio Grande area that my remarks will apply most closely to this specific area. According to one study, curanderos in south Texas refer to three levels of curanderismo: the material, the spiritual, and the mental. On the material level, the healer uses objects, words, and materials according to preset formulas and rituals. The patient may be cleansed, for example, by rubbing an egg all over his or her body, permitting the egg to take the patient's illness unto itself. Or specific herbs may be administered, depending upon the diagnosis of the malady. Or, as in the case of *susto* or fright, the patient may be stretched out on the floor in the form of a cross, covered with a sheet, and swept over with a broom, while the healer repeats a magico-religious formula.

In the spiritual level, the practitioner goes into a mediumistic trance, allowing other spirits to enter his or her body and act through it. The Pancho Villa ceremony described in Chapter Five exemplifies this level of curanderismo. Definitions can get extremely complicated here, as most materias—the women who channel the Niño Fidencio as will be discussed in the next chapter—do not consider themselves to be curanderas. Some materias are indeed curanderas, but that requires additional skills and different training.

In the fall of 1998, I had a long visit with the nephew of a man who had been an important curandero in the Lower Rio Grande Valley between 1940 and 1970. Although the uncle knew medicinal herbs well and would recommend them on occasion, he would never sell herbs. He operated mostly on the spiritual level. He had some sort of affiliation with an organization called the Universal Church of the Master. He had a special spirit named Coquito, who was very playful and would provide comic relief, lessening the tension that often permeated mediumistic sessions. Another spirit who helped the uncle was that of an Indian. He would not channel any known deceased person or saint, although he respected Don Pedrito's memory and would occasionally visit his shrine.

The curandero would perform three kinds of function, all in a private chapel at his home. He would offer private consultations four days each week. He would hold more formal Wednesday evening and Sunday noon services. After hymns and prayers, the lights would go off and he would go into a trance. Finally, he would hold small group séances. These latter sometimes included interested Anglo-Americans. In addition, he would take telephone calls at any time.

Although he never made a fixed charge for his services, he would accept contributions as they were offered. Sometimes these arrived by mail from places as distant as Chicago. He would occasionally drive to California, visiting patients and having sessions. These trips would not only pay for themselves, but he would come home with a bit of extra money, all from free-will contributions. This money allowed him to live decently and to support five nephews and nieces, even putting them through college. I got the impression of a hard-working, service-oriented, conscientious man who believed completely in what he was doing and who was depended upon in different ways by a large number of people.

In the mental level of curanderismo—the rarest of all—the curandero or curandera radiates healing energy directly from his or her mind toward the patient, thus effecting the cure. Three of the individuals discussed in this book—Teresita Urrea, Don Pedrito, and El Niño Fidencio—seem to have practiced healing at the mental level. All three were humble people who claimed (at least in the beginning, on Teresita's part) to have received their powers from God.

God, in the final analysis, provides most healing power, in the minds of those who participate in curanderismo. One receives a *don*—a gift or grace—for healing. (This word should not be confused with the honorific "Don," which is used before a man's first

Life-sized statue in the Don Pedrito Shrine.

name as a sign of respect, as in "Don Pedrito," or "Don Porfirio.") This don may come after one has been cured oneself, or it may come as a result of a vision in which one is told one has a calling. One goes through a process of learning or preparation, which can take years, and which often involves suffering, privations, or penance. Many curanderos and curanderas do not charge fixed fees, explaining that the gift of healing was freely given to them, and that it is their obligation to use it when called to do so. Free-will donations, however, are usually happily accepted.

It must be understood that the culture I have been describing, and indeed all of the beliefs and practices I deal with throughout this book, are neither uniform nor static. Mexico is a large and highly regionalized country, which can and does embody great cultural variation even within specific regions. Urban practices may well differ from rural practices. Local beliefs and practices may reflect those of some specific, local Indian culture. Beliefs can even vary from individual to individual. And people from every part of Mexico have come to or crossed the U.S./Mexico border and settled down, adding their regional cultures to the mixture already there. Furthermore, all living culture changes with time. Nothing in human life is static, on the border or elsewhere, with individuals or with groups. But these generalizations should at least provide a framework for the initial approaches to an important and complex aspect of traditional Mexican culture.

Espinazo, N.L.
F.S. Constantino
Abril 5 de 1928 –

D. Munguia Fot.
Hda. Chavez, Coah.

El Niño Fidencio, from
a 1928 photograph.

CHAPTER 7

EL NIÑO FIDENCIO

A Heart Filled with Compassion

Voy a cantar un corrido	I'm going to sing a ballad
por favor pido silencio	I request silence, please
voy cantando agredecido	I'm singing gratefully
me curó El Niño Fidencio	El Niño Fidencio cured me
Fuí soldado de caballo	I was a cavalryman
muy valiente y decedido	very brave and determined
pero una bala perdida	but a stray bullet
me dejo muy mal herido	left me very badly wounded
Me dijeron los doctores	The doctors told me
Que era difícil mi caso	That my case was difficult
Y entonces mi pobre madre	And so my poor mother
Me trajó aquí a Espinazo.	brought me here to Espinazo

Folk Saints of the Borderlands

These lines from the beginning of the *"Corrido del Niño Fidencio"* (the ballad of the Niño Fidencio) reflect the experiences of thousands of individuals on both sides of the border from the late 1920s to the present day, even though these verses were recorded (and presumably written) in 1927. A person is sick, and the doctors have not been able to help. But a cure is effected through the powers of a remarkable curandero who continues healing to this day, more than sixty years after his death.

José Fidencio Constantino Síntora was born in Iramuco, Guanajuato, in the fall of 1898. His parents were mestizos rather than Indians. We find conflicting traditions concerning his family: in some his father is named Socorro Constantino, while in others his father's identity is uncertain. He may have been one of a family of fourteen children or the fourteenth of twenty-five children! These details matter little to our story, but I mention them to show that El Niño, like the other individuals treated in this book, gathered legends and narratives about him. We do know he had a younger brother, Joaquín, however-er, who spent much of his life near Fidencio. By 1913, Fidencio was in Yuriria, Guanajuato, and assisted the local priest as altar boy. At the age of thirteen, Fidencio had started working as a kitchen boy for the local López de la Fuente family. He had attended school with young Enrique López de la Fuente, who probably took him north to work at the family hacienda at Espinazo, Nuevo León. There he stayed until his death in 1938, always in the company of Enrique López de la Fuente and accompanied by his younger brother.

According to legend, Fidencio at the age of eight set his mother's arm when she broke it in a fall. Later, at Espinazo, he showed great ability to treat animals and to assist at births, both animal and human. In other words, he became known as a *partero* or male midwife. He already had skill and reputation as a curandero, using herb remedies with deep understanding of their properties. He received the gift for this activity in a childhood vision, from a bearded man. The man, whom Fidencio believed to be Jesus, showed him a book containing many herbal cures, enabling Fidencio to cure his brother, who was sick at the time.

In Espinazo, however, came the vision that changed his life. It was three o'clock in the morning of August 15, 1927. Fidencio was sitting under a little *pirul* (pepper) tree, praying to "the celestial father" and contemplating human bitterness and suffering in contrast with God's love for humanity. He received instructions from Divine Providence to hold a large gathering on the nearby Cerro de la Campana on March 19, 1928. It was from this gathering that Fidencio's mission as a spiritual healer dates. (*Cerro de la Campana*—the Hill of the Bell—is a common name in Mexican topography. There is one such hill, for instance, in Hermosillo, Sonora, and a much more famous one outside the city of Querétaro, where the Emperor Maximilian was executed.)

At about this time, Fidencio met Teodoro von Wernich, a German-born Spiritist, and cured him of a previously incurable ulcer. In return, von Wernich promised to make El Niño famous. From that time on, von Wernich and López de la Fuente served as El Niño's advisors and publicists. Beginning in 1928, then, El Niño Fidencio grew in reputation as a healer.

THE CURES

Y hasta el Presidente Calles	And even President Calles
cansado de padecer	tired of suffering
cruzó montañas y valles	crossed mountains and valleys
y a Fidencio vino a ver.	and came to see Fidencio.

~from José Coronado Tovar's corrido "El Niño Fidencio," transcribed from a 1928 phonograph record

Mexico at this time was in chaos, with the Revolution coming to an end, and the federal government quite literally at war with the Catholic Church. In central and west Mexico, battles were fought, prominent individuals on both sides were assassinated, and priests were executed. (Many of these priests have since been elevated to sainthood.) Although the so-called Cristero War officially ended in 1929, scattered hostilities continued well into the 1930s. It was against this background of social and religious fracture and disruption that Fidencio played his highly public role as a healer. He performed his healings in front of hundreds, perhaps even thousands, of people. He welcomed reporters and freely talked with them. In fact, it was probably the spate of newspaper articles that appeared in Mexico City and elsewhere in 1928 that inspired the huge crowds who started arriving at Espinazo that year. Indeed, El Niño welcomed all comers. When Dr. Francisco Vela, vice-president of Nuevo León's state committee on public health, visited Espinazo in 1930, he was immediately ushered into El Niño's presence and then shown all over the area. Above all, El Niño encouraged people to photograph him.

These photographs exist in great numbers and are treasured and traded among Fidencio's followers today. Many show El Niño at work curing patients, and some even show him performing surgery with a bit of broken glass. One fascinating picture shows Fidencio sitting next to one of his patients after an apparently successful operation. A camera rests in his lap. Many of the pictures that show El Niño with his patients have captions written onto the photo in white ink. These photos have become the counterparts of the traditional ex-votos or *retablos* so common in Catholic countries in recent centuries. In these, the subject of the miracle is shown lying sick in bed or suffering an accident or even an assault, while the interceding saint or aspect of Christ hovers above and to one side. A text at the bottom explains the miracle.

Other pictures are portraits of El Niño—holding a puppy, posing with a child, dressed in riding boots and white riding breeches, or just looking somberly into the camera. El Niño reportedly loved children and animals. He also loved to dress up, and many of his costume changes were captured on film. He is most often shown, however, wearing either a white robe or white shirt and trousers, often with a white kerchief around his head.

In one story, a young boy, son of a Spanish immigrant, had suffered an accident with a firecracker that caused him to go gradually blind. His doctors held out no hope for him, so his parents took him on the two-week journey to Espinazo. There they camped for weeks in a brush shelter, waiting for El Niño. When they finally stood before the curandero, El Niño told the mother that there was no need to explain how the boy lost his sight. He massaged the boy's eyes for a few minutes with his fingers, then lifted his own eyes "as though he were having a vision."

El Niño Fidencio addressing a crowd. Photos such as this are sold at Espinazo and are collected in great quantities by Fidencistas.

After some time, El Niño lowered his head and continued massaging the boy's eyes. At last he said, "*Ya estás curado*" ("Now you're healed"). He requested that a handkerchief be brought and put over the boy's eyes until early morning light. Next morning, as the bandage was removed, the boy exclaimed, "*Ya veo*"—"I can see."

Another story tells of a man with chronic dyspepsia, to the point where the smell of food made him sick. After the doctors had given him up as hopeless, his wife went with him to Espinazo. The Niño entered their tent and, without asking any questions, began to massage the man's stomach. When he departed, Fidencio left a bunch of bananas to eat, even though the wife said that fruit made her husband very sick. However, the patient asked for a piece of banana, ate it and continued eating till he had consumed four bananas, at which point he was violently ill. The next day, El Niño massaged the man's stomach with a paste made from fruit, soap, and medicinal herbs. By the second day, the man had improved greatly, and by the fourth day, he walked for the first time in months.

Folk Saints of the Borderlands

In yet another account, a young man from Monterrey had gone insane, and his parents brought him to Fidencio. The healer extracted the young man's teeth. Following this, the young man regained his sanity. A doctor from Torreón who witnessed this, himself reported to have been cured of paralysis by El Niño, reasoned that an infection in the young man's teeth had affected his nervous system and caused the insanity. The grateful young man stayed in Espinazo to work in Fidencio's household.

Some of Fidencio's cures reveal a sense of playfulness. For instance, he led a deaf-mute near a swing and proceeded to swing back and forth, bumping the patient each time. The man became very angry and found his voice for the first time in several years. On another occasion, El Niño treated a paralytic by throwing sweets just out of her reach, forcing her to stand if she wanted to eat one of them. He would also perform "general cures," throwing food, tortillas, even eggs from the roof to the crowds below. Whoever was touched by one of these objects would be cured. He is said to have danced with people to cure them, and "given parties for his patients, prescribing herb baths, laughter, and foods." He made sure visitors to Espinazo were fed and entertained.

Perhaps El Niño's most famous cure involves Plutarco Elías Calles, president of Mexico between 1924 and 1928, and behind-the-scenes ruler until 1936. Here is the outline of the story as I heard it from a Fidencista in Robstown, Texas.

President Calles came to Espinazo on a special train with the intention of having Fidencio killed. Although President Calles was incognito, Fidencio recognized him without difficulty and knew why he had come. El Niño visited the president in his private car and said to him three times, "Do what you need to do." He then left and continued treating those who had come to see him. When Calles came to see Fidencio, he had to stand in line like everyone else. It was a hot day, and Calles was wearing a suit and tie. He pulled out his handkerchief to mop the sweat off his brow, forgetting that this was the prearranged signal for his men to shoot the Niño. However, they did not shoot, for a reason not mentioned in the story. Instead, Calles fainted and had a vision that seemed to identify Fidencio with Christ. When he came to, he was brought to Fidencio, where he fell on his knees, begging forgiveness. (The narrator here explained that Calles was a Mason, and Masons aren't supposed to kneel to anybody.) Fidencio commanded the president to strip, which he did, down to his underclothes. At that point it was discovered that Calles had leprosy. El Niño cured Calles of leprosy, but in exchange Calles had to make a truce between the government and the Catholic Church, thus bringing the Cristero War to an end. On another occasion, the archbishop of Mexico visited Fidencio incognito, apparently with ill intent. El Niño recognized him.

This is but one version of the Calles story. Others have it that Calles' sister was cured, sometimes of leprosy, or that his daughter was cured. Most accounts agree that after Calles' visit, El Niño received large quantities of supplies from the federal government. I have not heard or read elsewhere that El Niño was responsible for the agreement between church and state in Mexico, an agreement reached in 1927, and which is conventionally laid at the door of Dwight Morrow, then United States ambassador to Mexico. Readers familiar with European-derived folk tales will perhaps recognize several familiar motifs in this narrative: the importance of the number three, the disguised evil-doer recognized by the hero, and the accidental signal for execution. I find it comforting in a way to see such age-old narrative details attached to a story concerning happenings in twentieth-century Mexico.

That these stories exist in many different versions does not bother most Fidencistas. Different people have different knowledge, different versions of the stories, and different ways of performing their tasks. We hear many stories about Fidencio, just as we find many photographs of him. Discrepancies in details don't really matter, but the faith in El Niño is vital. It is shared by all and unites his followers.

The late 1920s and early 1930s were the heyday of El Niño's fame and popularity as a healer. At any given time in those years, several thousand people might have been camped at tiny Espinazo. I've heard that in 1928 and for a while afterward, more people purchased tickets for Espinazo than for any other destination in Mexico. A post office branch was opened to cope with the large quantities of mail that flowed into the community. Attempts were made to organize the site on orderly principles, with dirt streets being laid out and named. A room was dedicated for surgery, and another room held glass jars containing tumors that had been removed. These are still there. There was a maternity ward, a place set aside for the insane, a separate place for lepers, and a school. And there was also a cemetery for those El Niño could not cure. Accounts tell us that he recognized many of these cases upon their arrival before him, remarking to the crowd, "A person is coming who is wasting his time; tell him to go off and prepare for his death; I can't help him except to pray for him."

All this activity did not go unnoticed by the state health authorities. As Fidencio did not claim to be a doctor or prescribe medicines, the press stated, the authorities would not intervene. But they were deeply concerned about the health menace created by the thousands of sick, incurable, and dying people who were congregated in one place. During the last years of his life, Fidencio was under almost constant attack, first by the medical authorities, and later by the Catholic Church. He was twice arrested and taken before tribunals in Monterrey, but without a conviction. During this period, up to his death in 1938, his importance as a media figure declined, while his popularity with el pueblo—the common people—continued unabated.

What was this man like? Photographs and eyewitness accounts give us a fairly good picture. An article in *El Universal de México* for February 16, 1928, describes him as "a young man of few words, muscular, with a sort of yellowish color, and very simply dressed." Dr. Francisco Vela of the state of Nuevo Leon's committee on public health reported after his visit in 1930 that Fidencio looked serene and intelligent, and that he had a "rare," almost yellowish skin color. He also had "thick lips, a full set of large teeth, and light-colored eyes that chose to look away from the intruding eyes of visitors."

Indeed, in many of the photographs I have seen, El Niño is looking away from the camera. He had no visible facial hair, smooth skin, and a high-pitched voice. No sexual involvements with either men or women have been reported of him; he seemed asexual.

Although the Spiritists would have loved to claim him as one of their own, he denied contact with spirits of the dead, saying rather that his healing powers came as a gift from God. Often when healing he would go into a trance-like state, emerging with a cure for the patient he was working on. He had special powers of knowledge and could pick out individuals not known to him from a crowd. He would often work for days and nights without ceasing, sleep a few hours, and set to work again. He was abstemious in his habits, consuming mostly liquids. He usually dressed in a white robe or tunic and went barefoot. His living arrangements were simple in the extreme, consisting of a crude wooden bed, chair, and table. Even so, people say he preferred sitting and sleeping on the floor. He did not ask payment for his cures. Whatever food, supplies, or money were given him he redistributed among his followers. As he walked from place to place within his "hospital" at Espinazo, he was followed by a "healing circle" of hundreds of people.

I have given examples of some of his playful-seeming cures. Music and dance were important to him, and he encouraged both among his followers. Among the music heard in Espinazo were (and still are) songs—hymns, rather—in his praise. He also distributed fruits and candy, throwing them out among the crowds. The impression I gained from all the descriptions I have read and heard is of a sincere, uncomplicated, almost childlike man, deeply concerned for the suffering of others and equally deeply convinced of his healing mission.

During his lifetime he was already being compared to Christ. Like Christ, he healed and preached a message of love. Like Christ, he went to a nearby hilltop to meditate. Like Christ, he used water (in this case, from El Charco, the sacred pond at Espinazo) in ritual ways. And like Christ, he was expected to live for only thirty-three years. This would have put his death in 1931, but in fact he lived until October 1938, when he died just short of his fortieth birthday. His remarkable public career as a curandero lasted just ten years.

His death, like his life, has been surrounded by legend. Some of his followers believe that he, like Christ, died at age thirty-three, despite documentary evidence to the contrary. Many will tell you that he was killed by doctors who were jealous of his healing powers. El Niño told his followers he would go into a trance for three days and then arise again, they say. His spiritual qualities caused him to swell, however, and the doctors thought he was dead. They cut his throat to embalm him (or to perform an autopsy) and thus killed him. There are photographs of El Niño on his deathbed, surrounded by flowers. Others say that he hastened his own death from pernicious anemia by working for seventy-two hours at a time, hardly ever eating or resting. The extreme bloating of his body that occurred during his final trance or coma is attributed by some to the anemia, by others to his intense "spirituality that puffed him up," and by still others to the fact that he had been dead for a while in hot weather. He was buried, by special permit, some say, in his house, where his tomb is still visited by thousands of pilgrims annually.

FIDENCISMO

Whatever the cause and manner of his passing, El Niño Fidencio died in October 1938. In a very real sense, however, he still lives through his devotees. Some say that von Wernich taught him how to "project his spirit," and that before he died, he had trained some followers to take on his spirit. He is quoted as having said, *"Yo me tengo que morir, después de mi muerte vendrán muchos Niños Fidencios, pero recuerden que sólo hubo uno, y ese soy yo."* ("I must die; after my death there will come many Niños Fidencios, but remember, there was only one, and that is me.") This is interpreted by his followers to mean that he would manifest himself through many individuals. So many are needed because no one individual could contain his spirit in its entirety.

The individuals through whom Fidencio manifests himself are called *materias* and are to a great extent women. It is said that, although women were not El Niño's first choice, women's hearts are more disposed to accept him. More than sixty years after his death, men and women are still answering El Niño's call to be his voice for healing on this earth. El Niño chooses his materias, but does not force himself on them—they must give themselves to him willingly. The process of becoming a materia is similar to that of becoming a curandero. In each case the individual receives a calling and a don or gift. Curanderos, however, receive their calling and their don from God, while materias receive theirs directly from El Niño. A materia may also be a curandera, but this is a different, independent gift. Materias are empowered only to allow El Niño to work through them.

After being called by El Niño, a man or woman receives guidance from an experienced materia. Preparation includes sacrifice, prayer, meditation, and often physical penance. Becoming a materia is not easy: El Niño is described as looking for big hearts so that his heart can come through them to all the other hearts that suffer. At one time the materias-in-training were expected to go to Espinazo and be quizzed while in a trance state by the elders of the movement. As the oldest generation of Fidencistas dies off, this is no longer as important as it once was.

The groups of Fidencistas who follow a particular materia are called *misiones*—"missions." There are misiones all over the Texas borderlands and even as far west as California. Misiones gather in a special room or building—often called a *templo*—set aside for El Niño's service. In this room stands an altar called a *trono* or "throne." Usually, a trono will have one or more busts or large photographs of El Niño in a central location, flanked by artificial flowers and other religious pictures. There is usually at least one crucifix, perhaps other representations of Christ, and images of a number of saints. Prominent among these is the Virgin, especially in her aspect as Our Lady of Guadalupe.

Folk Saints of the Borderlands

El Niño had great respect for women, especially his own mother, and a strong devotion to the Virgin of Guadalupe. In fact, some followers referred to him during his lifetime as "El Niño Guadalupano." At his autopsy, people say, an image of Guadalupe was found stamped on his heart. (This is not the only sacred image fixed on Fidencio's body. His hard palate bore the impression of a crucifix, and this was used to make wax impressions for the faithful.) One famous photograph shows El Niño Fidencio, clad in white robes and a red cloak and pointing to his flaming heart, in the guise of the Virgin of Guadalupe. He stands on a black crescent moon supported by an angel, just as the Virgin does, and is surrounded by the same aureole of flames and bunches of roses. While this image has caused consternation among some non-Fidencista Catholics, most Fidencistas apparently feel it to be appropriate.

During a typical healing ceremony, the materia goes into a trance and becomes El Niño, or "Niñito," as many of his followers affectionately refer to him. Dressed in a white robe with a red cape or sash, the materia speaks in a high-pitched voice, saying and doing whatever El Niño wishes. Many of the curing activities are those used in life by El Niño: walking on patients, throwing fruit and candy to supplicants, and the like.

The fiesta days, October 17 and 19 (observed as El Niño's birth and death dates) and March 19 (the day of San Jose or Saint Joseph, his patron saint), see a huge influx of the faithful into Espinazo, a tiny semi-deserted village for the rest of the year. Every year, thousands of pilgrims from both sides of the border arrive in Espinazo by train and automobile. They camp in and around the village. They visit the various sacred sites: the pirulito tree where Fidencio received his defining vision, the hill where he would meditate, the *charquito* or pond where he would treat lepers. Above all, they visit the hacienda containing the room where he worked, where he saw Jesus walking, and which is the site of his tomb. And all the time, in a hundred different bodies and guises, El Niño himself is present: healing, advising, distributing candies as he did in life, consulting.

Materias are not limited to channeling El Niño exclusively. Other spirits who work through them may include Teresita Urrea, Pancho Villa, and others, including a little girl named Aurora.

While many Fidencistas see no conflict between their Fidencio-related beliefs and activities and their status as good Catholics, *Fidencismo* has been established as a separate religion and is officially registered as such in Mexico. This has resulted in a split in the movement between those who consider themselves Fidencistas and those who consider themselves Catholic Fidencistas. The headquarters of Fidencismo is Espinazo, the site of Fidencio's work in this life.

A VISIT TO ESPINAZO

I visited Espinazo on March 16, 2003, a few days before the saints' day fiesta for San Jose that would take place on the nineteenth. As soon as we turned off Mexico's Highway 53 onto the paved road to Espinazo, we became aware of El Niño. A monument consisting of a curved concrete slab and several tall poles stands to one side of the road junction. A central pole supports a crucifix, with a bust of El Niño a bit farther down on a pedestal. Lower, flanking poles support flags, with eagles and angels set on pedestals between them. Attached to the pole on the far left of the assembly is an openwork, two-dimensional wire sculpture of El Niño himself, with his hands partially raised in blessing.

As we turned off the main highway, we passed a group of pilgrims dressed in white, walking toward Espinazo. A few kilometers farther down the Espinazo road lies a hot spring, which on the Sunday we drove by was crowded with Fidencistas. A chapel dedicated to both El Niño Fidencio and El Señor del Camino had a constant stream of pilgrims walking in and out. An arch decorated with artificial flowers stood by the road at the entrance of the path to the chapel. Halfway down the path stood a six-foot-tall column topped by a gold bust of El Niño. The column was painted lavender, and sculptured vines twined up its sides, while the bust was dressed in a long red cape and a white baseball cap. Beyond it was the chapel, also painted lavender, with relief vine decorations similar to those on the column. To one side stood a small monument commemorating the "crowning" of

El Charco, the sacred pond in Espinazo. A materia, flanked by two assistants, is effecting the cure of the man in front of her. (March 2003)

El Niño Fidencio on October 17, 1988. It was dedicated by a *misión* in Matamoros, Tamaulipas, and bore a symbol we would encounter in several more places as well: the sun rising over a mountain with a cross silhouetted in front of it. Beyond the chapel and to the left lay the hot spring. All the time we were there, people were entering and leaving the area.

The road into Espinazo was lined by the largest number of religious monuments—nichos and the like—that I remember ever seeing along a road in Mexico. Some were dedicated to conventional saints and to the Virgin in one or another of her manifestations; others were dedicated to El Niño. Many of the latter bore dedicatory plaques from a specific misión. Close to town, an entryway had been erected over the road by the Iglesia Fidencista Cristiana, with a sign welcoming pilgrims.

Once we parked our car and walked across the railroad tracks on the edge of Espinazo, we were met by a scene of great activity. To the left of the entrance road stood a statue of El Niño wearing a polo costume and carrying a riding crop. The statue was painted white except for the boots, a belt, the crop, and a bow tie, which were black. On the other side of the road within a metal fence stood El Pirulito, the sacred pepper tree where El Niño had received his don. Also within the fence was a *nichito* or small shrine. As we arrived, a group of traditional *matachines* were dancing to music provided by a large drum. They were led by two older women and wore red shirts, stockings, and fore-and-aft aprons to which were attached rows of cane segments that made a rustling noise as they danced. They were surrounded by a circle of men and women of all ages, holding hands. All of these wore shirts bearing the legend on the back MISIÓN NANCY/MONCLO-VA, N.L. Associated with this group was a materia working on a young man who was kneeling in front of her. When she (or El Niño, who was working through her) finished with him, a young woman took his place.

As we watched the matachines, an entire misión marched past us, head-ed out of town and across the tracks. They were led by their materia, who was dressed in white robes and red cape, and by a banner carrier.

The street going into the tiny town was lined with booths selling all sorts of goods: tools, commercial cookware, clay pots and bowls from further south in Mexico, clothing, toys, and secular and sacred souvenirs. Among the latter we saw Fidencista cassettes and CDs (two whole booths were devoted to these), Fidencista songbooks and books about El Niño, prayer cards to many saints, El Niño T-shirts and shopping bags, and countless photographs of the famous curandero. Most of these were historic photos from Fidencio's lifetime, but we also saw doctored photos showing the Virgin of Guadalupe comforting El Niño (a theme that also appeared on T-shirts), Christ blessing El Niño, and the Holy Family with El Niño stand-ing by. One surprise was the presence of a large number of photographs of Pancho Villa—chatting with associates, leading charges, riding his horse, posing with Emiliano Zapata on the presidential throne. Apparently Villa has also become a popular individual for materias to channel.

A lot of food was sold at the fiesta. I saw candy booths; one booth sell-ing beautiful, decorated loaves of bread from Tlaxcala; and booths selling barbecued chicken, *menudo, gorditas,* tostadas, and red tortillas that had apparently been dipped in chile. Drinks available included sodas, various homemade drinks, and beer.

Through all this commercial hubbub came the pilgrims, often organized in misiones and led by a materia. One such group walked slowly up the street toward Fidencio's tomb in a circle with hands linked, singing hymns as they came. Within the circle were two women, going slowly on their knees. Others were led by their materias, often in trances, supported by a woman on either side, with the group dressed uniformly, carrying a banner, and singing hymns.

Toward the end of the street stood a large white building—the hacienda. It contained El Niño's tomb—a focal point for many of the processions. Groups were standing by the tomb, praying and singing. Others drifted through the house, viewing the room where Fidencio had slept and the murals depicting incidents in his life, purchasing religious souvenirs, praying. Behind the house in a garden stood the swing El Niño had used in some of his cures. I was offered the opportunity to sit in it, and the young woman who showed it to me seemed disappointed that I didn't choose to swing more vigorously than I did. (I weigh 260 pounds, though, which might have affected my decision not to do so.)

Past the building stood the charco. It was full of people while I was there—groups smearing each other with black, sticky, curative mud, materias and their attendants working with

Booth in Espinazo with Fidencista and other devotional materials for sale. (March 2003)

patients, other people just relaxing in the curative waters. On the road out of the village we encountered groups of dripping pilgrims, their clothes and faces black with mud, sloshing their way back to their temporary dwelling places. So much activity, and the actual fiesta was still three days off!

On the road out of town, we passed under the same arch we had seen earlier. From this side the sign read FELIZ VIAJE Y DESEAMOS QUE HALLAN ENCONTRADO EL ALIVIO Y LA PAZ QUE BUSCABAN ("Happy journey and we hope you have found the relief and the peace that you sought"). It was signed "Iglesia Cristiana Fidencista." As we

Roadside monument to El Niño Fidencio, between the main highway and Espinazo.

drove off, we started to muster our impressions of this incredibly vibrant scene. Much of it was like most other Mexican religious fiestas we had attended. One thing, however, stood out—this was an intensely happy gathering. All the people were enjoying themselves in a particularly gentle way—apparently the spirit of El Niño was at work in more ways than simply through his chosen materias.

Except for fiesta times in Espinazo, Fidencismo is not a very public religion. There are no Fidencista shrines along the roads aside from the stretch I described, and Fidencista ceremonies are performed in homes or in templos especially dedicated to that use. Aside from the occasional pictures of El Niño that one can encounter in south Texas *botánicas,* one doesn't see many signs of this highly popular religion. But it *is* highly popular, and definitely a force to be reckoned with in the total picture of health care and spirituality along the border.

Portrait of Father Kino by Sonoran artist Nereo de la Peña, inside the dome over Kino's gravesite in Magdalena, Sonora. (March 1998)

CHAPTER 8

MORE SAINTS,
More Stories, More Thoughts

A FEW POTENTIAL SAINTS

The figures we have been looking at are the major non-canonical saints I have found in the U.S.–Mexico borderlands. Many other minor ones exist, of course, and the list of these keeps changing, as individuals such as Pedro Blanco in Nogales, Sonora, are forgotten and others rise in popularity.

One person whose posthumous career I have been tracing with some interest is Luis Donaldo Colosio, an extremely popular and charismatic young politician from Magdalena, Sonora, who was the presidential candidate of PRI, the ruling party at that time, until his assassination in Tijuana in March 1994. At one time a few years ago it seemed that he would join the ranks of folk saints in the region. A maker of frames for holy pictures near Magdalena created several moving assemblages in tribute to him. One woman of my acquaintance, a professional seller of medicinal herbs, told me that she kept such a picture on her home altar and prayed to Colosio whenever she went into the back country to gather medicines. (She confided with a shy smile that she prayed to Mother Teresa as well.)

A few poems of tribute were placed with the floral offerings at Colosio's tomb when I visited there. (The tragedy and its sentimental potential were intensified when his lovely young wife died of cancer within a year of his death.) But I have neither found nor heard of ex-votos, candles, or ribbons being placed in any number at either his tomb or his death site in Tijuana, which the PRI has turned into a monument. I have been told that flowers are indeed brought to Colosio sites on the anniversary of his death, but these may well be tributes or remembrances rather than offerings. Statues of him abound, especially in Sonora, and Colosio campaign signs, along with black mourning bows, are maintained in his hometown of Magdalena. But all this sounds more like the commemoration of a beloved political figure than the veneration of a saint. I have been told that his father, who survived him, has been very discouraging of signs of veneration and devotion. Perhaps when this man dies… But perhaps not.

In the oldest cemetery of the seaport city of Guaymas, Sonora, stands a handsome neoclassic chapel. It marks the resting place of Presbítero Francisco Navarrete, brother of Archbishop Juan Navarrete and a particularly beloved priest. Father Navarrete was born in Oaxaca in 1888 and died in 1940. During the period of religious persecution in the middle 1930s, he stayed in Sonora, hiding in the towns of Guaymas and Empalme. He served the faithful as best he could as a clandestine priest, while his brother the archbishop took to the hills and organized a more active program of resistance.

People say that during the active persecution of the 1930s, Padre Francisco disguised himself by growing a moustache and wearing overalls. During a period of heavy rains and flooding in Empalme, a train struck a poor man, bringing him to death's door. An apparently humble passenger jumped off his second-class bench, landed on the ground, and pushed his way through the crowd of spectators. He administered confession and applied the holy oils to the dying man, then vanished once more into the crowd. It was Padre Francisco, risking capture to perform his priestly duties.

Padre Francisco died on March 14, 1940, in Guaymas, where he was a parish priest. His last words are said to have been "Sweet Mother of Sorrows: if my life is necessary in order that these souls be saved, here it is." I was told in Hermosillo, at the small museum dedicated to his brother, Archbishop Juan, that Padre Francisco was known by the people of Sonora to be a saint. Implied but not stated was the notion that there was no need to seek an official statement from the institutional Church on that subject—his people knew it already. At his chapel I saw two ex-votos thanking him for miracles rendered.

Statue of the late Luis Donaldo Colosio in the *plaza monumental* of Magdalena, Sonora, on a spot where the murdered candidate gave an important address. (October 1997)

A similar attitude is taken by many Catholics in Buffalo, New York, toward their local saint. In that city, a beloved priest named Father Nelson Baker (circa 1842–1936) founded orphanages and schools, cared for the sick and homeless, and fed the hungry. He is especially remembered for his charitable work during the Great Depression. He, too, is locally considered a saint, and legends are told about miracles he performed. I have been told that his although his devotees would prefer his sainthood to be recognized by the Vatican, they know he is in Heaven and act accordingly.

SERRA, KINO & MARGIL

Three historical figures along the border are currently being promoted for sainthood. All three were missionaries in the eighteenth century. They are Fray Junípero Serra, O.F.M., in California; Father Eusebio Francisco Kino, S.J., in Arizona and Sonora; and Fray Antonio Margil, O.F.M., in Texas. They present an interesting contrast to the figures with whom this book is primarily concerned.

Junípero Serra was born on the island of Mallorca in 1713. Ordained a priest at seventeen, he was a professor of theology at twenty-two. In 1749 he traveled to New Spain and walked all the way from Vera Cruz to Mexico City. In 1767 he was assigned to head the Franciscans who replaced the recently expelled Jesuits in Baja California, and the next year he was assigned to explore and found missions in Alta California, now the state of California. Serra spent the rest of his life in California, founding nine missions before his death in 1784. (To "found a mission" is to establish a program for the conversion of peoples. Building a church is a separate activity that may follow the founding of a successful

Prayer card to Fray Junípero Serra.

mission.) He was known for his iron willpower and his enthusiastic mortification of his flesh.

Serra was beatified by Pope John Paul II in 1987, but has yet to be canonized. His beatification caused considerable protest among Native American activists and others, who considered Serra to have been overly harsh with the Indians under his control. As yet uncanonized, Serra remains an important but controversial figure in California history.

Eusebio Francisco Kino, S.J., was a pivotal figure in the history of the Pimería Alta, the region that would become northwestern Sonora and southwestern Arizona. Born in 1645 in the northern Italian village of Segno, Kino became a Jesuit as a result of promises he made while suffering from a potentially fatal disease as a young man. After training in mathe-

Statue of Fray Margil at Mission San Juan, south of San Antonio, Texas. (September 1998)

matics, astronomy, and cartography, he went to New Spain, where he worked for a while in an unsuccessful mission program in Baja California. In 1687 he started his work in the Pimería Alta. An indefatigable traveler, he established twenty missions in this region, introducing wheat farming and cattle-raising to the area at the same time. To this day, much of the traditional diet in northern Sonora and southern Arizona is based on wheat and beef. He died in 1711 in the mission community of Magdalena, which he had founded, and was buried there.

Kino's bones were uncovered by a team of archaeologists in 1966 and remain in their original site, visible under glass in the midst of a monumental plaza—a plaza created in Kino's honor a few years later. Jesuits working in both Mexico and the United States are campaigning for formal recognition of his sainthood, so far without official results.

Fray Antonio de Jesús Margil was born in 1655 in Valencia, Spain, and entered the Franciscan order in 1673, in his native city. He arrived in Mexico in 1683 and had a long and varied career in Mexico and Guatemala, working with native peoples and founding colleges, before his arrival in Texas in 1716. He founded the mission of San José de Aguayo south of San Antonio in 1720 and died in 1726. He called himself "God's Donkey" because he could walk faster than a mule, and his staff is believed to have miraculously sprouted vines. The Church named him "Venerable" in 1836, but his cause has not materially progressed since then.

All three of these historical figures' causes continue to have support by members of their religious orders. I have seen prayer cards printed to Kino and Serra; I have not found one addressed to Fray Margil. I have not found any of these cards for sale in botánicas or other venues serving a basically working-class Catholic clientele. My impression is that their devotees, with few exceptions, are educated Catholics in the border region with some interest in history. Kino may be a partial exception to this generalization; milagros are occasionally placed near his burial site, and I have seen one ex-voto statement written on a piece of cardboard propped against a statue of him at a busy Tucson intersection.

A Few Last Words

To return to our six folk saints—what, if anything, do they have in common? In the first place, although all are venerated as saints within their communities, none has even a remote possibility of being formally recognized as such by the Catholic Church. All exist outside of the formal religious system. All were in some way marginal to mainstream Mexican society even in their day, and only Don Pedrito seems to have been admired or even tolerated by the establishment. All, except for Teresita, seem to have been poor or at least raised in poverty. Teresita, Don Pedrito, and El Niño Fidencio lived lives filled with service to others. Even Villa and Malverde can be said to have served the needy by distributing stolen goods to them. Only Juan Soldado has no established legend of service to the poor, although the few comments concerning his interest in children may represent the beginnings of such a legend.

Villa, Juan Soldado, and Malverde died dramatic and violent deaths at the hands of a hostile establishment, and Juan's followers are quick to point out the parallels between his life and that of Jesus. Fidencistas, as well, believe that their El Niño shared many characteristics with Jesus. He healed the sick and threatened the powerful, which latter group might have had him killed. Although documents show that he died at age forty, some of his followers believe that he, like Jesus, only lived for thirty-three years. Moreover, he has returned and is constantly returning to this world as materias channel him for healing purposes.

Traditional regional folk religious customs show through in the cases of some of the six. An example of this is the emphasis placed on rocks and rock piles in the stories concerning Juan Soldado and Jesús Malverde. In each case, a rock pile was created at the place of death, as has been common practice in northwest Mexico for hundreds of years. And in each case, rocks and pebbles are used in the devotional practices.

I was telling a priest about my research one day, and, after recounting the story of St. Martin of Tours and the spurious martyr, I remarked that Mediterranean Catholics seem to have been venerating social bandits for some sixteen hundred years. "Yes, and they'll keep on doing it as long as the Vatican only canonizes members of religious orders and goody-goodies!" was the somewhat unexpected response. The point is a good one, especially given Mexico's strong class system, its traditional anticlericalism, and its deep suspicion of bureaucracy, be it secular or church-related. As the Mexican poet Octavio Paz put it, the only things Mexicans really believe in are the Virgin of Guadalupe and the National Lottery.

Most important, perhaps, is the fact that these ánimas or folk saints, or whatever they should be called, produce results. Many people pray to them or go to séances in which they are channeled because they have "come through" for friends or relatives. Most of these people do not have access to many of the sources of power—be they medical, legal, or economic—available to their more fortunate contemporaries. All lives are filled with uncertainty, and none more so than those of folks who for one reason or another must exist on the fringes of mainstream society.

In the case of Malverde, we find an additional factor. He operated outside the law and perhaps will approve of others who do so, as long as they use some of their profits to help their communities. If one needs to get a load of heroin across the border or rub out the opposition, as one friend told me, there's no sense in asking for help from the Virgin or the Holy Family. That's not what they do. But such activities are part of the world that Malverde occupies, and these experiences seem to indicate to his believers that he understands and will help. In other words, if it works, try it.

For example, I know of an older, very devout Catholic woman from Sonora. When her son discovered that she had visited the Malverde chapel in Culiacán, he asked her why she had done so. Her response was, "Why not? It can't hurt anything, and it may help."

This pragmatism, in the final analysis, goes far to explain the importance of the figures whose stories appear in this book. They seem to supply hope if not help to many who stand in most need of those commodities. Like those who petition them for help, they stand outside the mainstream of society, at odds in one way or another with the bureaucracies of both church and state. In most cases, the establishment has treated them badly, just as it is perceived to have mistreated many of those who come to them for help. But they have been shown to possess power and to bring that power to the poor of the borderlands, who are often striving to cope with not one but two hostile systems. That is their strength; that is why they endure and shall probably continue to do so for many years to come.

Map of the BORDERLANDS

A Brief Look at Mexican History

Mexico has seen three great periods of armed struggle, all three of them referred to in this book. First came the **Spanish Conquest,** in the course of which the territory that is now Mexico became part of the Spanish Empire under the name of New Spain. A famous event during this period was **La Noche Triste** or "the night of sorrows," on June 30, 1520, when the Spanish conquistadors were forced to flee the Aztec capitol of Tenochtitlán with all their accumulated loot. The Aztecs discovered their plans, and after extremely heavy fighting, the surviving Spaniards were lucky to get away with their lives.

The **War of Independence** lasted from 1810 until 1821, when Mexico finally broke loose from the Spanish Empire, of which it had been part since the sixteenth century. Although the **Royalists** fought to remain attached to Spain, the **Insurgents** finally succeeded in establishing an independent Mexican state.

The **Mexican Revolution** occurred in several stages from 1910 until 1928. In its early phases, it was an armed reaction to the thirty-year dictatorship of President **Porfirio Díaz,** familiarly referred to as **Don Porfirio.** Díaz, a conservative "strong man," encouraged outside investment in Mexico through the occasionally brutal repression of any kind of labor movement—whether in the mines, the factories, or on the great haciendas. His rule is known as the **Porfiriato.** After Díaz' exile to France in 1911, the Revolution became a power struggle between various remaining factions.

The revolution against Díaz was started by **Francisco I. Madero,** a scion of a wealthy family from Coahuila in northeast Mexico. Madero, also well-known as a Spiritist, was murdered in 1913 on the orders of **General Victoriano Huerta,** who succeeded him as president. Opposition to Huerta immediately formed in northern Mexico under the leadership of

Venustiano Carranza. The Constitution of 1917 was written during his time in power. Carranza was killed in turn while trying to escape Mexico City in 1920, and he was succeeded by Pancho Villa's old enemy, the Sonoran **Álvaro Obregón. Emiliano Zapata** was southern Mexico's great agrarian revolutionary leader. Zapata's field of influence was strongest in the state of Morelos, south of Mexico City. He was murdered by federal forces in 1919. His name has been borrowed by the current indigenous revolutionary movement in the southern state of Chiapas.

The **Cristero War** was a bitter religious conflict that divided much of Mexico in the 1920s and 30s, between Mexican government forces and Catholic guerrillas whose rallying cry was *"Viva Cristo Rey"* or "Long Live Christ the King." Because of this cry, the guerrilla forces were called **cristeros,** loosely translatable as "soldiers of Christ." The root causes of the struggle were the anti-religious attitudes of the socialist revolutionary government of Mexico as expressed in the Constitution of 1917, compounded by the extreme conservatism of the Mexican Catholic hierarchy at the time.

Some Definitions

ánima soul or spirit

Aztlán the mythic origin place of the Aztecs, identified by the Chicano movement as the American Southwest

barranca a ravine, gorge, or steep-walled dry wash

botánica a store specializing in curative herbs, but also selling prayer cards, candles, other religious articles, and materials associated with *curanderismo*; a *yerbería*

capilla a chapel

carreta a cart

Chicano/Chicana movement a political and social movement that began in the 1960s in the U.S. Southwest; Americans of Mexican descent chose their own identifying labels (the word "chicano" derives from "Mexicano") and began to forge their own literary and cultural identity, part of which included the concept that the border states were Aztlán, the mythic homeland of the Aztecs

comadre, compadre one's co-godmother or co-godfather—the godparents of one's child, for example

corrido a Mexican ballad; a narrative song in Spanish

curandera, curandero a female or male folk healer

curanderismo the field of traditional Mexican folk healing

doctor of the Church a saint who is recognized by the official Church for his or her learning and holiness of life

Don preceding a man's first name, a title of respect, often used with older men and in some sense the equivalent of using Mr. before the last name in English; **Doña** is the equivalent for women

don a gift or grace, such as the power to heal people

ex-voto a thanks offering left at a shrine or altar, often visually symbolizing in some way the nature of the miracle received; can include plaques, pictures, or *milagros*—the original Latin phrase means "according to a vow"

Fidencistas followers of El Niño Fidencio

Guadalupana, Guadalupano the adjectival form of Guadalupe (the Virgin of Guadalupe is often called *La Guadalupana*); "El Niño Guadalupano" refers to the image of El Niño Fidencio given the same artistic treatment afforded the Virgin of Guadalupe

hacendado land owner

la ley fuga, also **la ley de fuga**
literally, "the law of flight": the
once-common Mexican practice of
shooting prisoners "while trying to
escape," often after having forced
them to dig their own graves; la ley
fuga is often associated with the
Porfiriato

Marian having to do with the Virgin
Mary—for instance, a **Marian
monogram** is a design incorporating
the Virgin's initials

matachines ritual dancers who do a
European-derived contra dance in
two long lines, usually as an act of
devotion to some saint

materia a Fidencista medium, usually
a woman; male mediums are
sometimes called *cajones* (which also
means "large containers")

Mayo a Native American group
belonging to the Cáhitan language
family, living on the coastal plain of
southern Sonora and northern Sinaloa

milagro a miracle; also a small metal
image, usually depicting a part of
the body, often pinned to a saint's
image in petition or in thanks for
the miraculous healing of the body
part represented

milagro concedido miracle granted

misión, misiones the name for a
Fidencista congregation

narco, narcotraficante a member of
the drug-trading world

narcocorrido a corrido about drug
dealers, growers, and smugglers,
usually treating them as heroes;
narcocorridos are an important
popular music form in northern
Mexico and the southwestern
United States

narcosanto, narcosantón the narco
saint, the big narco saint—in other
words, Jesús Malverde

nicho a niche, either built into a wall
or freestanding, usually containing a
religious image of some sort; a
nichito is a smaller nicho

novena a Catholic prayer cycle that
lasts nine days

palacio municipal the municipal
palace, or the seat of government
for a Mexican *municipio*, roughly
equivalent to a county in the
United States

ramada from the Spanish
enramada—an arbor or roofed
shelter without walls, often made of
boughs and branches

ranchera, canciones rancheras
ranch-style songs, a Mexican
equivalent of classic Country
Western songs, aimed at country
people living in the city, coping
with the sorrows and frustrations
of modern life

retablo the highly ornamental sculpted
surface behind an altar in a church
or chapel; may also denote a small
painting, which may or may not be
an ex-voto

romería a pilgrimage or a gathering of
people at a pilgrimage destination

santo as a noun, a saint; as an adjective,
"holy"; **santa** is the feminine form

soldadera a female volunteer soldier or
camp follower during the Mexican
Revolution; while most soldaderas
simply followed the army to cook
and care for their men, some were
armed and actually fought in battles;
the famous Mexican song "Adelita"
is about a soldadera; soldaderas have
become an important part of the
imagery of the Revolution

soldado a soldier

Sonorenses Sonorans, just as
Chihuahuaenses are people from
Chihuahua, and Tamaulipecos come
from Tamaulipas

Spiritism a religious system developed
by nineteenth-century Frenchman

Alan Kardek, revolving around the
belief that the spirits of the dead
may be communicated with;
Spiritists are followers of this system

Spiritualism a religious system
involving the invocation of spirits
as aids in curing; **Spiritualists**,
followers of this system, usually
function comfortably within the
context of Catholicism, although
communication with spirits is
denounced by the official Church

Tohono O'odham "the Desert
People," a Native American tribe
occupying the desert lands of
southern Arizona and northern
Sonora; formerly known as Papago
Indians

Yaqui a Native American tribe whose
homeland is in southern Sonora,
near Ciudad Obregón; closely
related to the Mayos, they were at
war with the Mexican government
through much of the late nineteenth
century; there are now also Yaqui
communities near Tucson and
Phoenix in southern Arizona

yerbería a botánica, or a store that
sells medicinal herbs, prayer cards,
candles, and other materials for the
practice of curanderismo

Sources

CHAPTER 1

Bahr, Donald. "Pima–Papago Christianity." *Journal of the Southwest* 30, no. 2 (summer 1988): 133–167.

Broderick, Robert C. *The Catholic Encyclopedia*. Huntington, Indiana: Our Sunday Visitor, Inc., 1975.

Cahill, Thomas. *Pope John XXIII*. New York: Viking Penguin, 2002.

Flandreau, Charles Macomb. *Viva Mexico!* London: Eland Books, 1982 (first published in 1908).

Forbes, Robert H. *Crabb's Filibustering Expedition into Sonora, 1857*. Tucson, Arizona: Arizona Silhouettes, 1952.

Griffith, James S. *Beliefs and Holy Places: A Spiritual Geography of the Pimería Alta*. Tucson, Arizona: The University of Arizona Press, 1992.

———. "A Diversity of Dead Helpers: Folk Saints of the U.S.–Mexico Borderlands." *Worldviews and the American West: The Life of the Place Itself,* Polly Stewart, Steve Siporin, C. W. Sullivan III, and Suzi Jones, eds. Logan, Utah: Utah State University Press, 2000.

Gruzinski, Serge. *Images at War: Mexico from Columbus to Blade Runner (1492–2019)*, trans. Heather MacLean. Durham, North Carolina: Duke University Press, 2001.

Holler, Stephen. "The Origins of Marian Devotion in Latin American Cultures in the United States." *Marian Studies* XLVI (1995): 108–127.

Ingham, John. *Mary, Michael, and Lucifer: Folk Catholicism in Central Mexico*. Austin, Texas: The University of Texas Press, 1985.

Katz, Friedrich. *The Life and Times of Pancho Villa*. Palo Alto, California: Stanford University Press, 1998.

Paredes, Américo. *A Texas–Mexican Cancionero: Folksongs of the Lower Border*. Urbana, Illinois: University of Illinois Press, 1976.

Quinones, Sam. *True Tales from Another Mexico.* Albuquerque, New Mexico: The University of New Mexico Press, 2001.

Spicer, Edward H. *The Yaquis: A Cultural History.* Tucson, Arizona: The University of Arizona Press, 1980.

Starr, Frederick. *Catalogue of a Collection of Objects Illustrating the Folklore of Mexico.* London: The Folk-Lore Society, 1899.

Toor, Frances. *Mexican Folkways.* New York: Crown Publishers, 1949.

Wald, Elijah. *Narcocorrido: A Journey into the Music of Drugs, Guns, and Guerrillas.* New York: Rayo (Harper Collins), 2001.

CHAPTER 2

Cabeza de Vaca, Vincent, and Juan Cabeza de Vaca. "The 'Shame Suicides' and Tijuana." *Journal of the Southwest* 43, no. 4 (winter 2001): 602–635.

Griffith, James S. *Beliefs and Holy Places: A Spiritual Geography of the Pimería Alta* (Chapter 3: "A Saint and His People"). Tucson, Arizona: The University of Arizona Press, 1992.

———. *A Shared Space: Folklife in the Arizona–Sonora Borderlands* (Chapter 4: "El Tiradito and Juan Soldado: Two Victim-Intercessors of the Western Borderlands"). Logan, Utah: Utah State University Press, 1995.

———. *Saints of the Southwest.* Tucson, Arizona: Rio Nuevo Publishers, 2000.

O'Connor, Anne-Marie. "Unlikely Saints." *The Albuquerque* (New Mexico) *Journal,* August 9, 1997. Reprinted from the *Los Angeles Times.* The article has appeared in different newspapers under different headlines.

Toor, Frances. *Mexican Folkways.* New York: Crown Publishers, 1949.

Valenzuela Arce, José Manuel. "Por los milagros recibidos: religiosidad popular a través del culto a Juan Soldado." ed. Valenzuela Arce, José Manuel: *Entre la magia y la historia: tradiciones, mitos y leyendas de la frontera.* Tijuana, Baja California Norte, Mexico: Programa Cultural de Fronteras, Colegio de la Frontera Norte, 1992.

Vanderwood, Paul. "Juan Soldado: Field Notes and Reflections." *Journal of the Southwest* 43, no. 4 (winter 2001): 717–727.

CHAPTER 3

Note: The details of the historical narrative come from Holden (1978) and Vanderwood (1998).

Broderick, Robert C. *The Catholic Encyclopedia.* Huntington, Indiana: Our Sunday Visitor, Inc., 1975.

Holden, William Curry. *Teresita.* Owings Mills, Maryland: Stemmer House, 1978.

Kelly, Isabel. *Folk Practices in North Mexico: Birth Customs, Folk Medicine, and Spiritualism in the Laguna Zone.* Austin, Texas: The University of Texas Press, 1965.

Kelly, Sean, and Rosemary Rodgers. *Saints Preserve Us.* New York: Random House, 1993.

Lamadrid, Enrique. "El Corrido de Tomochic: Honor, Grace, Gender, and Power in the First Ballad of the Mexican Revolution." *Journal of the Southwest* 41, no. 4 (winter 1999): 441–460. (The two lines quoted from verse eleven come from this source.)

Lowe, Charlotte. "Queen of the Yaquis: The mystical story of his great-aunt, the healer Teresita, beckons author Luis Alberto Urrea." *The Tucson* (Arizona) *Citizen,* April 29, 1994.

Lowe, Sam. "Saint Preserve Us: Clifton resurrects the legend of Teresita." *The Arizona Republic* (Phoenix, Arizona), March 25, 1996.

Madsen, William, and Claudia Madsen. *A Guide to Mexican Witchcraft.* Mexico City: Minutiae Mexicana, S.A. de C.V., 1972.

Negri, Sam. "Teresita, the Saint of Cabora." *Arizona Highways* 70, no. 3 (March 1994): 13–14.

Newell, Gillian Elizabeth. *Teresa Urrea: Early Chicana? The Politics of Representation, Identity, and Memory.* University of Arizona master's thesis, 1999.

Vanderwood, Paul. *The Power of God against the Guns of Government: Religious Upheaval in Mexico at the Turn of the Nineteenth Century.* Palo Alto, California: Stanford University Press, 1998.

Wilson, Hattie. "Teresa Urrea's fame teetered between witch and saint." *The Nogales* (Arizona) *International,* September 10, 1986.

CHAPTER 4

Álvarez Nolasco, Ernesto. *1956: Flor y Espina de Sinaloa*. Culiacán: Archivo Histórico General del Estado de Sinaloa, 2002.

Butler, Alban. *Butler's Lives of the Saints,* Vol. II. London: Burnes and Oates, 1981.

Cantrell Gamboa, Melvin. "Malverde y Bernal, el santo y el héroe." In *Historia de la violencia, la criminalidad, y el narcotráfico, memoria del XVII Congreso de Historia Regional, versión internacional*, 129–136. Culiacán, Sinaloa, Mexico: Instituto de Investigaciones Económicas y Sociales, Universidad Autónoma de Sinaloa, 2002.

Escobedo, Helen, and Paolo Gori. *Mexican Monuments: Strange Encounters*. New York: Abbeville Press, 1989.

García S., Luís Antonio. "Malverde: leyenda de un bandido milagroso." *Crónicas* 1, no. 1 (2002): 1–21.

Grant, Richard. "At the Shrine of the Narcotraficantes." *Esquire Magazine* (British edition, September 1995).

Griffith, James S. *Saints of the Southwest*. Tucson, Arizona: Rio Nuevo Publishers, 2000.

Hernández, Guillermo E. *The Mexican Revolution* (178-page booklet accompanying the four-CD set of the same name). El Cerrito, California: Arhoolie Records 7041–7044 (1996).

Kelly, Sean, and Rosemary Rodgers. *Saints Preserve Us*. New York: Random House, 1993.

Lechuga Bórquez, Pablo. "San Judas Tadeo Vs. Malverde." *El Independiente* (Nogales, Sonora), May 5, 2000.

Lizárraga Hernández, Arturo. "Jesús Malverde, ángel de los pobres." *Revista Mar y Arena*. Culiacán, Sinaloa, Mexico: Universidad Autónoma de Sinaloa, Facultad de Ciencias Sociales (as seen at www.maz.uasnet.mx/maryarena/noviembre98/jesusmal.html in June 2003).

López Sánchez, Sergio. "Malverde, un bandido generoso." *Fronteras* 1, no. 2 (1996): 32–40.

Mejía Madrid, Fabrizio. "Tiempo fuera: el lamento de Malverde." *La Jornada Seminal* (September 26, 1999), as seen at www.jornada.unam.mx/1999/sep99/990926/sem-mejia.html.

Mercado, María Luisa. "Malverde, el santo de los narcos, visitado por militares y politicos." *La Crónica de Hoy* (Mexico City), August 3, 1997 (www.mit.edu/people/aaelenes/sinaloa/narco/malverde/malverde7.html, as seen June 2002).

Ochoa Vega, Alejandro. *The State of Sinaloa* (guidebook). Culiacán: Estado de Sinaloa, 1997.

Quinones, Sam. "Jesús Malverde—Saint of Mexico's Drug Traffickers May Have Been Bandit Hung in 1909." Pacific News Service, www.int.edu/people/aalenes/sinaloa/narco/marverde/malverde5.html (as seen June 2002). (The quotation from DPS Sergeant Manny Flores comes from this article.)

————. *True Tales from Another Mexico.* Albuquerque, New Mexico: The University of New Mexico Press, 2001.

Sánchez, Ray. "Mexico's Drug Lords Find Patron in Thief Turned Saint." *The Seattle* (Washington) *Times*, February 26, 1997.

Silverman, Leigh, and Sam Quinones. "Drug Lord." *The New Times* (Phoenix, Arizona), February 11–17, 1999.

Wald, Elijah. *Narcocorrido: A Journey into the Music of Drugs, Guns, and Guerrillas.* New York: Rayo (Harper Collins), 2001.

Walsh, Michael, ed. *Butler's Lives of the Saints.* San Francisco, California: Harper and Row, 1987.

Woodward, Kenneth L. *Making Saints.* New York: Simon and Schuster, 1990.

CHAPTER 5

Behar, Ruth. *Translated Woman: Crossing the Border with Esperanza's Story.* Boston, Massachusetts: Beacon Press, 1993.

Gruzinsky, Serge. *Images at War: Mexico from Columbus to Blade Runner (1492–2019),* trans. Heather MacLean. Durham, North Carolina: Duke University Press, 1991.

Hernández, Guillermo E., trans. *The Mexican Revolution* (178-page booklet accompanying the four-CD set of the same name). El Cerrito, California: Arhoolie Records, CD 7041–7044, 1996. www.arhoolie.com

Hobsbawm, Eric. *Bandits.* New York: The New Press, 2000. (Hobsbawm's definition of social bandits is found on page 20.)

Johnson, William Weber. *Heroic Mexico: The Narrative History of a Twentieth Century Revolution.* New York: Harcourt Brace Jovanovich, 1968 (rev. ed.).

Katz, Friedrich. *The Life and Times of Pancho Villa.* Palo Alto, California: Stanford University Press, 1998.

Mendoza, Vicente T. *El Corrido Mexicano.* Mexico: Colección Popular del Fondo de Cultura Económica, 1954.

Schmitt, Jean-Claude. *The Holy Greyhound: Guinefort, Healer of Children Since the Thirteenth Century.* Cambridge, U.K.: Cambridge University Press, 1983. (The story of St. Martin appears on pages 22–23.)

CHAPTER 6

Note: The historical material in this chapter comes from the first two works listed.

Brooks County Historical Survey Committee. *The Faith Healer of Los Olmos— Biography of Don Pedrito Jaramillo.* Falfurrias, Texas, 1990. (The passage from a "local church bulletin" comes from page 4.)

Dodson, Ruth. "Don Pedrito Jaramillo, the Curandero of Los Olmos." In *The Healer of Los Olmos and Other Mexican Lore, Publications of the Texas Folklore Society, Number* XXIV, ed. Wilson M. Hudson. Dallas, Texas: Southern Methodist University Press, 1984. (The quotations attributed to the doctor and the parish priest are found on page 16.)

Kelly, Sean, and Rosemary Rodgers. *Saints Preserve Us.* New York: Random House, 1993.

Malagamba Ansótegui, Amelia. "Don Pedrito Jaramillo, una leyenda mexicana en el sur de Texas." *Entre la magia y la historia: tradiciones, mitos y leyendas de la frontera,* ed. José Manuel Valenzuela Arce. Mexico City: Programa Cultural de las Fronteras, el Colegio de la Frontera Norte, 1992.

Paredes, Américo. *A Texas–Mexican Cancionero: Folksongs of the Lower Border.* Urbana, Illinois: University of Illinois Press, 1976. (The verses of the song "Don Pedrito Jaramillo" quoted in this chapter were translated by Paredes and come from pages 120–121.)

Rodriguez, Liborio. "Tata Pedrito, Rasgos Biográficos, Versificados." Broadside poem in 26 verses purchased at the Don Pedrito Shrine, Falfurrias, Texas (n.d.).

Thompson, John. "Santísima Muerte: On the Origin and Development of a Mexican Cult Image." *Journal of the Southwest* 40, no. 4 (winter 1998): 405–436.

Torres, Eliseo. *The Folk Healer: Mexican–American Traditions of Curanderismo.* Kingsville, Texas: Nieves Press, n.d.

Trotter, Robert T. II, and Juan Antonio Chavira. *Curanderismo: Mexican–American Folk Healing.* Athens, Georgia: The University of Georgia Press, 1997.

CHAPTER 7

Note: Most of the historical material in this chapter is drawn from Garza Quirós (1991) and Spielberg and Zavaleta (1998).

Anonymous. "Corrido del Niño Fidencio," from *Canciones y Alabanzas al Niño Fidencio,* n.d. A version of this corrido was recorded by Los Trovadores Tamaulipecos in New York on June 6, 1929, and issued as "Niño Fidencio" on the OKEH label as OK 1624.

Gardner, Dore. *Niño Fidencio: A Heart Flung Open.* Santa Fe, New Mexico: Museum of New Mexico Press, 1992.

Garza Quirós, Fernando. *El Niño Fidencio y el Fidencismo.* Monterrey: Editorial Font, S.A. (Quinta Edición), 1991.

Macklin, Barbara June, and N. Ross Crumrine. "Three North Mexican Folk Saint Movements." *Comparative Studies in Society and History* 15, no. 1 (January 1973): 89–105.

Spielberg, Joseph, and Antonio Zavaleta. "Historic Folk Sainthood along the Texas–Mexico Border." *Studies in Matamoros and Cameron County History,* Milo Kearney, Anthony Knopp, and Antonio Zavaleta, eds. Brownsville, Texas: The University of Texas at Brownsville and Texas Southmost College, 1998. (The quotations describing Fidencio's appearance may be found on page 367.)

Torres, Eliseo. *The Folk Healer: Mexican–American Traditions of Curanderismo.* Kingsville, Texas: Nieves Press, n.d.

Tovar, José Coronado. "El Niño Fidencio." Recorded by Cancioneros de Sonora in New York, ca. August, 1928, and issued as Columbia 3258. Also recorded by Enriqueta Almazán y Pompeyo Benavides in San Antonio, Texas, on May 25, 1928, and issued as Victor 81239A.

Vidaurri, Cynthia. "Las Que Menos Quería el Niño: Women of the Fidencista Movement." *Chicana Traditions,* Norma Cantú and Olga Nájera, eds. Urbana, Illinois: The University of Illinois Press, 2002.

CHAPTER 8

Anonymous. "Junipero Serra (1713–1784)." *New Perspectives on the West.* www.pbs.org//weta/thewest/people/s_z/serra.htm (as seen in November 2002).

Bantjes, Adrian A. *As If Jesus Walked on Earth: Cardenism, Sonora, and the Mexican Revolution.* Washington, Delaware: Scholarly Resources, 1998.

Brading, D.A. *Mexican Phoenix: Our Lady of Guadalupe: Image and Tradition across Five Centuries.* Cambridge, U.K.: Cambridge University Press, 2001.

DeZavala, Adina. *History and Legends of the Alamo and Other Missions in and around San Antonio.* Houston, Texas: Arte Público Press, 1996.

Fish, Lydia. "Father Baker, Legends of a Saint in Buffalo." *New York Folklore* X, nos. 3–4 (Summer–Fall 1984): 23–33.

Jarboe, Jan. "Mission Accomplished: San José." www.texasmonthly.com/ranch /mission/mission3.php (as seen in November 2002).

Olvera H., Jorge. *Finding Father Kino.* Tucson, Arizona: The Southwest Missions Research Center, 1998.

Polzer, Charles W., S.J. *Kino, A Legacy: His Life, His Works, His Missions, His Monuments.* Tucson, Arizona: Jesuit Fathers of Southern Arizona, 1998.

Sugranes, Rev. Eugene, CMF. "Margil was 60 Years Old when He Founded Mission Here." *San Antonio* (Texas) *Express,* February 22, 1931 (as seen at http://alamo-de-parras.welkn.org/archives/newsearch/amargil.html in November 2002).

Acknowledgements

This book is the work of many more people than the one whose name appears on the title page. I have discussed the project with, asked questions of, sought (and occasionally taken) advice from, and gone on field trips with a large number of friends, whom I wish to thank here. Richard Morales has been a dear friend and introducer to his culture for more than thirty years. He was with me when we first learned about Juan Soldado; his understandings and quiet respect provide a constant example for me. Bernard Fontana, former teacher, valued colleague, and good neighbor, has suffered through statements of despair and enthusiasm in roughly equal proportions. Cynthia Vidaurri has generously put her deep understanding of the Lower Rio Grande border country and of traditional Mexican medico-religious beliefs and practices at my service. Father Thomas J. Steele, S.J., and Father Gregory Adolf increased my understanding of Catholic doctrine and beliefs. Erika Brady listened to a lot of half-formed ideas and offered sage advice. My wife, Loma, put up with a lot and provided the structure that allowed the book to start to happen.

For much of the fieldwork involving Juan Soldado, I was accompanied and greatly helped by Richard and Carmen Morales and Loma Griffith. Antonio Federico of Tucson and his cousin Francisco Federico of Oquitoa, Sonora, provided information concerning El Chapo Charo. Licenciado Francisco Javier Manzo Taylor of Hermosillo and R. P. Guillermo Coronado of Ures took me to the shrine of El Arrastradito in Opodepe. Manzo also took me to the grave of Father Navarrete in Guaymas and told me some of his story. He and José Rómulo Felix accompanied me to the grave of Carlitos el Milagro. Mario Munguía of Hermosillo accompanied me to the Museo del Arqueobispo Navarrete. Finally, Alfredo Gonzales was with me on my visit to the shrine of El Difunto Leyva—a visit facilitated by John Klingeman of the Museum of Big Bend at Sul Ross University in Alpine, Texas, and Bennie Joe Gallego of Sul Ross Library. Carlos Rohana of Ojinaga accompanied us to the shrine, and ex-Presidente Municipal Victor Sotelo of the same town also offered information. Dr. Felipe de Jesús Valenzuela of Magdalena, Sonora, offered insights into Juan Soldado and victim-intercessors in general.

Charles Spezia of Clifton was a generous host on one of my trips to that town in search of Teresita's grave. Barbara Kingsolver answered questions about her experiences during the Clifton miners' strike. Francisco Manzo was my companion on my trip to Cabora. Professor Heriberto Aja of Hermosillo allowed me to copy the hymn to Teresita pasted inside the cover of an old book, and José Rómulo Felix of the same city shared with me what his father had told him concerning Don Tomás Urrea and his famous daughter. Judge Eileen Hollowell and Mary Beth Dawson told me the story of the Teresita chapel in Cascabel, Arizona. Luis Alberto Urrea, a collateral descendant of Teresita, shared information concerning his famous relative. Dr. Felipe de Jesús Valenzuela shared a photo of Teresita in his possession.

Folk Saints of the Borderlands

The late Arturo Carrillo Strong told me much about Malverde and some of the relevant customs of the narcotraficante world. This study would have been much better had we been able to visit the shrine together as we had planned. Celestino Fernández and Cynthia Vidaurri visited Malverde's shrine and brought me materials and information. Ross Humphreys and Alfredo Gonzales of Tucson and Francisco Manzo of Hermosillo, Sonora, were my companions on visits to various other Malverde sites in Sonora and Chihuahua. Rosalita Ayala of Tucson deepened my understanding of Malverde in a number of ways. José Rómulo Felix of Hermosillo organized my visit to the Malverde Chapel in Culiacán, Sinaloa.

In Culiacán, I was privileged to interview Dr. Rigoberto Rodríguez B. of the Departamento de Historia of the Universidad Autónoma de Sinaloa, as well as Gilberto López Alanís, director of the Archivo Histórico General del Estado de Sinaloa, the actor Hector Monje, and author Elmer Mendoza. At the shrine itself, we were graciously received by Sra. Teresita Sánchez and by Jesús Manuel González Sánchez, son of the chapel's long-time custodian.

Alfredo Gonzales visited Parral and la tumba de Villa with me. While in Parral we learned much from several older gentlemen whose names we neglected to learn.

Cynthia Vidaurri helped me toward a better understanding of Don Pedrito. Her husband, Lane Fauch, accompanied me on my first visit to the shrine at Falfurrias, while my wife, Loma Griffith, accompanied me on a much later visit. Descendants of Don Pedrito's adopted son kindly answered my questions in the Don Pedrito store. Adán Benavides helped me toward a better understanding of curanderismo in South Texas.

Cynthia Vidaurri and Lane Fauch once again helped me better understand Fidencismo and put me in touch with Doña Nieves Reyes Aguiñada of Robbstown and her son, both of whom graciously granted me interviews. Cynthia generously shared her vast store of printed materials with me. Chris Strachwitz of El Cerrito, California, made available three 1928 recordings of corridos about El Niño Fidencio. Alfredo Gonzales of Tucson, that excellent traveling companion, visited Espinazo with me.

Norma Cantú and Paul Vandermark read early versions of the first chapter and offered suggestions and encouragement. Cynthia Vidaurri read the manuscript in its entirety and offered helpful comments, as did Alfredo Gonzales. My wife, Loma, read it several times and offered the suggestions that led to its final form. Were it not for her I might still be floundering in a state of dull unreadability.

These people I have named. There are literally scores of others whose names I never knew who have provided information throughout the project. All have contributed to what is good in this book; responsibility for the mistakes is mine alone.

Index